T0195884

PREVIOUS BOOKS

SPIRITUAL WISDOM FOR PEACE ON EARTH
From Sananda
Channeled through David J Adams

LOVE is the **KEY.** Part 1
Spiritual Wisdom from Germain
Channeled through David J Adams

LOVE is the **KEY.** Part 2
Spiritual Wisdom from Germain
Channeled through David J Adams

WE ARE ALL ONE
Spiritual Wisdom from The Masters of Shambhala
Channeled through David J Adams

ENLIGHTENMENT AND ILLUMINATION
Spiritual Wisdom from Djwahl Khul
Channeled through David J Adams

COSMIC SYMPHONY OF LOVE
Spiritual Wisdom from Hilarion
Channeled through David J Adams

THE NEW EARTH
Spiritual Wisdom from The Merlin, Ar'Ak and
Spirit of Crystals and Gemstones
Channeled through David J Adams

GATEWAY OF LOVE
Spiritual Wisdom from Tarak, Dylanthia, Margot, Neptune
Channeled through David J Adams

HARMONY OF HEALING THROUGH CRYSTALS BY SPIRIT OF CRYSTALS AND GEMSTONES

David J Adams

authorHOUSE®

AuthorHouse™
1663 Liberty Drive
Bloomington, IN 47403
www.authorhouse.com
Phone: 833-262-8899

Published by AuthorHouse 09/20/2021

ISBN: 978-1-6655-3833-6 (sc)
ISBN: 978-1-6655-3831-2 (hc)
ISBN: 978-1-6655-3832-9 (e)

Library of Congress Control Number: 2021919164

The Front Cover Painting is a representation of Spirit of Crystals and Gemstones painted and photographed by Kaye Ogilvie, Intuitive artist from Queensland, Australia.

Back cover Photo was taken on the camera of David J Adams, the T shirt was created by Tie Dye artist, Ruth Cary Cooper from USA.

Print information available on the last page.

CONTENTS

DEDICATION

I Dedicate this book to my children, Nicky and Suzi, my grandchildren, Lauren, Matthew and Emily, and my great grandchildren, Ruby–Rae and Peyton, for they and others of the next generations will carry the Light forward and create the Peace that we all yearn for.

ABOUT THE AUTHOR

ADAMS, David John Patrick
Born: 28th April 1943
At: Mountain Ash, Glamorgan, South Wales, UK.

Lived 3 years in Karachi, Pakistan, and 2 years in Egypt, before moving to South Australia in 1971.

Currently living in the southern suburbs of the city of Adelaide.

Came to his path of awakening in late 1987, quite probably as a result of the energy of the Harmonic Convergence in August of that year.

Was quickly introduced to the beautiful world of Crystals, and joined a group called Crystal Consciousness - which shortly thereafter became "EarthMother" - under the leadership of Heather Niland.

In 1991, he was asked by Beloved Master Germain to undertake a global Meditation based on, and working with, the Consciousness of the Oceans, to be called the Marine Meditation. This was to be held at 8pm on each Equinox wherever people were in the world. The Marine Meditation was held each Equinox from March 1991 to September 2012 – some 44 Meditations in all,

He continues to work both with Crystals and the Oceans. He attended a gathering of Masters in new Zealand in 1996, a healing Summit in Glastonbury, UK in 1998 and a healing Summit in Sth Molle, Queensland in 2000. In 2009 he was asked to address a Peace Conference in Istanbul to speak of the Marine Meditation and his work for World Peace through meditation.

He is a songwriter, a musician, a writer of Musical Theatre productions and Author of the book "The Earthmother book of Energy based Healing" – now out of print - but more important, a SERVANT OF PEACE.

David began bringing through information from a variety of Masters and Cosmic Beings in the form of Meditations around 1991, particularly a series of Meditations from the Spirit of Crystals and Gemstones. It was not, however, until after the year 2000 that he began to channel messages in group situations and in individual sessions. Most of these messages were not recorded or transcribed so remain shared with only a few people, but in 2009 the messages being brought through in the weekly Pendragon Meditation group began to be recorded and transcribed by Kath Smith and sent out around the world on David's own Pendragon network. The disseminating of the audio versions of these messages did not begin until 2012.

David's special Guide and Mentor has been 'The Germain, the I am that I am', but he has also worked extensively with – and channeled - Hilarion, Djwahl Khul, AA Michael, The Merlin, The Masters of Shambhala, as well as Arcturian Sound Master Tarak and his own Home Trinity Cosmic Brother Ar'Ak.

Contact email – djpadams8@tpg.com.au)

ACKNOWLEDGEMENTS

I, David J Adams, would like to acknowledge three special Earth Angels.

Heather Niland/Shekina Shar - who helped me to awaken to my Journey in 1987 and connected me to my Beloved Friend "The Germain", she also connected me to the wonderful Crystal Dimension. she was a mentor, guide and teacher way ahead of her time.

Meredith Pope – who walked in the same shoes as me in those difficult early years as a fellow 'weekender' at The EarthMother Centre where Spirit of Crystals and Gemstones first connected with me. Meredith was - and still is - an inspiration to me.

Kaye Ogilvie, Intuitive Spiritual Artist from Queensland, who 'Tuned in' to Spirit of Crystals and Gemstones and produced the image that adorns the front cover of this book.

BLESSINGS OF LOVE, JOY AND PEACE TO EACH AND EVERY ONE OF YOU.

DAVID J ADAMS

FOREWORD

From the Dawn of recorded history, Crystals and Gemstones have played an important role in the ritual, the fashion, the wellbeing and the Spirituality of the Human race. Although the specific focus of their connection may change from time to time, they are ever present in their Harmonious relationship with us, however, due to these changes of focus, much Wisdom and information relating to them has been lost or overlooked through the ages.

As we move from a focus of fashion and adornment into a focus of healing and Spiritual awakening, much ancient Wisdom relating to Crystals and Gemstones is being re-discovered or 'remembered' through our connection with 'Pure Consciousness'.

Crystals and Gemstones are **'of the Earth'** and contain within them the accumulated knowledge of time spans beyond our imaginings. To connect with them is therefore to open yourself to a world far beyond that which you see or touch, far beyond that which you can measure or categorize. **You will be undertaking a journey of Personal Growth that will transcend the limitations of Third Dimensional existence.**

But all journeys have to have a beginning, and I hope within this Book to provide you with that beginning. I hope to awaken in you the first spark of understanding that Crystals are more than mere 'rocks', that first spark of interest in learning **MORE** about Crystals and Gemstones, and through your association with them, more about **YOURSELF !!**

WELCOME TO THE BEAUTIFUL WORLD OF CRYSTALS AND GEMSTONES.

LET THE JOURNEY BEGIN !!

INTRODUCTION

"Greetings, I am Spirit, Spirit of Crystals and Gemstones"

These special words begin each meditation in this series, which covers 19 Special Crystal Beings, and when they first came through me I was filled with the most powerful, yet infinitely gentle, energy that I had ever experienced. I had reached one of those moments in my journey of growth that marked a shift to a new level of awareness, that moment when you know that it is time to leave the nest that has nurtured your growth so far, and reach out to embrace your next stage of growth. I felt the fear and the self doubt wash over me, and I asked for help from the Hierarchy of Light. Immediately this energy of incredible Love swept over me, and the words flowed into my being,

"Greetings, I am Spirit, Spirit of Crystals and Gemstones. I come before you in true Light and

Infinite Love to share and guide your exploration of the wondrous beauty of my Earthly Children, the Crystals"

I was then taken on the first of my 19 journeys into the embrace of our brothers and sisters in the Crystal Dimension, to the special warmth and healing of the beautiful Amethyst. It was no accident that the Amethyst embrace was the opening experience, imbued as it is with the Violet Flame, as it has become increasingly clear to me that Spirit of Crystals and Gemstones is one of the many facets of the energy of the beloved Master Germain. A Guide and Master that I had already worked with on other projects.

It is hard to explain how these meditations came through me, I was not in a **'trance state'** and I did not **'visualise'** what was taking place. It was as if there was a sudden, complete, **"Knowing"**, accompanied by that incredible energy of Love, and the words manifested in my mind. As quickly as one was written down there seemed to be another waiting to embrace me, although why it ended with just 19 Crystal experiences I do not know to this day. I had worked with Crystals, both in meditations and in healing situations previously, but through

Spirit came a new and deeper **ONENESS** with them, it was as if in the moment of **"knowing"**, I literally **'became'** the Crystal that was embracing me. A profoundly moving – I could even say, life changing – experience. I only hope that I have been able to capture in some small way the majesty of the experiences that Spirit of Crystals and Gemstones shared with me, and that the reader/listener too will find Joy and Growth in the gentle, loving embrace of our Crystal brothers and sisters, as they share their words and feeling with you in meditation.

To commence each meditation you need to hold a piece of the appropriate crystal in your left hand, and adopt a relaxed position in a quiet place. These meditations can be enjoyed in solitude or in a group situation and do not require any specific ritual beyond that which you would normally use, or are comfortable with. Each crystal type is unique, but each crystal within the same type is also unique, even though they share similar qualities. Each crystal shared will therefore create a special interaction with your own uniqueness as a Being of Light. So, put away any preconceived ideas of what particular crystals "do" or "mean", just let yourself flow into the waiting arms of the crystal through the essence of Spirit, **AND EXPLORE YOURSELF !**

You will find relaxation within these meditations because they are brought to you by Spirit in the gentle, soothing vibration of **LOVE**. You will find healing within these meditations, the natural healing that evolves from a greater understanding of your own multi-faceted and multi-Dimensional Being. But I hope you will find growth and a new awareness within them also, awareness of the partnership that we as humans have with all the other various life forms that co-exist on this beautiful Planet called **EARTH.** Crystals are themselves **'living entities'**, **'Beings of Light'** who reach out to us in Light and Love that we might work together with mutual Honour and Respect for the Highest Good of **ALL**. That we may, **together**, create a world united in **PEACE, LOVE and HARMONY**.

Blessings be upon you

David J Adams

1

HARMONY OF HEALING THROUGH CRYSTALS PART 1 : AT - ONE - MENT WITH CRYSTALS

"MY ESSENCE CAN NOT BE CAPTURED EASILY ON PAPER

FOR WORDS ARE MERE FRAGMENTS OF KNOWING,

AND I AM CONSCIOUSNESS ITSELF"

Most people come to Crystals with the perception that Crystals are inanimate objects. Exquisitely sculptured works of art within nature, but essentially lifeless chunks of rock.

Many people, even among the ranks of "Crystal Healers", or "Crystal workers", never leave this perception. They acknowledge and accept that crystals have the capacity to receive, store and emit energy, and that Crystals vibrate at particular frequencies. But this, of itself, does not equate in their thinking to what is normally considered "Life". This is because mankind, in its arrogance, defines "life" purely in terms of reflected aspects of itself !

I hope within this sharing to lead you to a different perception, and therefore a different way of relating to and working with Crystals.

Through my work with the Spirit of Crystals and Gemstones – an energy of Consciousness that came to me some years ago to share a greater awareness of Crystals - I have come to realize that Crystals are living Beings with their own consciousness. Indeed, they are Souls experiencing an Earthly manifestation, just as we are Souls experiencing an Earthly manifestation. They have simply chosen to have a different Earthly form and Earthly experience than we have.

If this seems a little wild and improbable, remember this, the Human body can be dissected, analyzed and categorized, but science has yet to establish a method by which it can prove the existence of a "Soul" or "Spirit". This vital quality, which is our very aliveness, can not be described within the framework of our limited human definitions. Spirit is by its very nature indefinable. Never the less it exists. So it is with Crystals !

If one accepts this perception of Crystals as "Incarnate Souls". it dramatically changes the way you relate to and work with Crystals. They can no longer be regarded as "Tools", and you do not "use" them. Instead, you need to establish a loving relationship with them, communicating with them as you would with a close friend, and establishing an understanding between the two of you about the work you have to do together. You will be contributing to the growth of the Crystal as much as the Crystal will be contributing to your growth.

Since I was brought to this understanding, and have opened myself more fully to the "Soul" aspect of Crystals I have been amazed at the power and clarity of the interaction. I am still unable to describe how the communication occurs, I only know that it does, and in healing and meditation there is a feeling of being part of a group consciousness that was not there before. Indeed, at one stage during my time at Spirit of Crystals Healing Centre, crystals participated in our meditations to an amazing extent, to the point of dictating their own lay outs on the table around which we meditated, and these lay outs added a new dimension to the meditation experience !!. I have also experienced a cluster of Madagascan Blue Celestite divide into two smaller "Soul" clusters - as I held the large cluster in my hands - One "Soul" cluster introduced itself as 'Neptune', and was to work with us on the Marine Meditation, and the other as 'Aquarius', which was to go with Meredith Pope (partner in Spirit of Crystals at the time) into her new home.

Seek to form a mutually respectful relationship with the Crystal. The first step in this is to be prepared to "Listen" to the Crystal, ask how it can best work with you rather than assuming that it will do your bidding. You do not do things "to" Crystals, you do things "with" Crystals. Allow yourself to be guided as much by the Crystal as by your own desires.

Begin by paying attention to your imagination, since Crystals speak to us through non verbal images, body sensations, Heart feelings and "ideas" that pop into our minds as we hold the Crystal.

Then, we need to go back to basics, to the very beginning of our connection with a particular Crystal and re - write the script. It is certainly true that crystals choose you as much as you choose a crystal, but how can this be so ? Unless, of course, the Crystal has a consciousness of its own ! The choice to come together is mutual, and involves a need for growth that each can contribute to the other. You will often see that when people seek to bring a Crystal into their lives, they hold their hands over it, or lift it to their ear. Are they seeking to establish that the Crystal has a powerful energy field, or that it has a vibration that resonates comfortably with their own ? Most often this is the case, but this makes a judgement on a crystal that is fundamentally flawed, since it deals only with the periphery energy of the crystal, and fails to establish the crystal's purpose or role within the person's life. I would suggest that the only valid way to bring a crystal into your life is to pick the crystal up and "ask" if there is a contribution that you each have to make to each other's growth.

Having "agreed" to share a part of our journey of growth with a particular crystal (by whatever means), why is it that our first move with a new crystal is to cleanse it ? We are not dealing with any impurities or problems within the crystal, because we haven't bothered to find out if there are any. We make an assumption, and that assumption is rooted within our own fears. We are afraid that we may pick up some negative energy or entity that has attached itself to the crystal at some stage during its formation, its mining, or its passage through many hands to us. I wonder how the crystal is reacting to that, does it have the same irrational fears ? Is it silently screaming out to you to take a shower ! "Cleanse yourself before you handle me", "go and bury yourself in the ground for a few days, then come back and touch me". Sounds silly doesn't it ? Yet, are we any the less silly for directing those same comments to the Crystal ?

Time to change that first move ! Sit in a quiet place with your crystal, take it in your hand gently and embrace its energy with a feeling of pure Love. Thank it for coming into your life at this time, and ask it if there is some special task that you have to do together. Ask the crystal if there are any disharmonious energies that need to be dealt with before you can work together, then ask yourself the same question - it is certain that the crystal is doing just that, because it is a mutual coming together !!

If there are disharmonious energies to be dealt with, ask the crystal to suggest an appropriate method. Don't be at all surprised if it comes into your mind to take a shower with your crystal for a mutual cleansing !!

Disharmonious energies DO exist, and can be picked up by Crystals just as they can be picked up by you. This is not a cause for fear, it is a natural part of "being alive". It can also be addressed simply and effectively by asking for the Violet Flame of Transmutation to be at the essence of your Being, and inviting your Crystal to do the same. Ask that all energies flowing to you (or the crystal), through you (or the crystal), and originating within you (or the crystal) be transmuted into "balanced Love and Light". It is a personal belief of mine that we should not ask for "negative" energies to be transmuted into "positive" energies, because I believe that this simply replaces one imbalance with another. What we should always seek to achieve is a state of balance. Crystals are also about "Balance", and are constantly guiding and inspiring you towards balance. Go with the flow !

Many crystals come to you with specific knowledge stored in them for your benefit or for the benefit of the work you have to do together, that could easily be lost if you ignore this "asking" process and make an assumption that cleansing is necessary - a bit like chucking a new garment in the washing machine without first checking if it's colour fast !

One word of warning at this point. Don't work or play with crystals if you are afraid of change or growth, because transformation towards the LIGHT is what crystals are all about. They may work through different aspects of your life to achieve this, but they will always be moving you in that direction.

When you have "broken the ice" and established a respectful communication with your crystal, you can then establish the role that you are to play together. Not all crystals will come into your life as partners in healing, and you should not be disappointed if they indicate that their specialty lies elsewhere. Just as all humans are not drawn to the field of healing, so it is with crystals. In whatever role they have in your life it is important to honour, respect and thank the crystals before, during and after working with them. Not because the crystal needs our thanks, but because the very process of "thanking" opens up something in us that's healthy and necessary for "our" Spirits.

Let us assume for the purposes of this sharing that the crystal that has come into your life has done so to work with you in the field of healing, what are the options? and where do you start? Once again, sit with your crystal and "ask" for information and guidance. Try to establish firstly if the crystal is to contribute to your personal healing or is to work with you in a healing situation with others. Then seek to establish if the crystal prefers to work indirectly or directly. A crystal may contribute to your personal healing in an "indirect" way simply by being worn or carried or placed close by you at home. Once again the crystal will be able to help you establish the most appropriate means by which the most beneficial interaction can occur. A crystal may contribute to your personal healing in a "direct" way by being placed on your body or moved over and around your body in a deliberate and conscious healing session. Again, "ask" the crystal for guidance.

There is no incorrect way to work with Crystals. The only thing you can do wrong is to approach Crystals with the intention of doing harm in any way. Do your crystal work only with positive, life affirming intentions, using your own spontaneity, creativity, and most importantly, the Divine (unconditional) Love within you.

It is important at this point to recognize that in working with a crystal in a healing situation - personal or otherwise - you are working with a flow of energy between two or more living, complex, Beings. Energy is not static, but is in a constant state of flux and motion. Within ourselves, therefore, we are constantly moving between balance and imbalance, integration and dis-integration, health and disease. We are not static creatures, but are dynamic energy essences, and our physical bodies process dynamic energy as does the crystal itself. The crystal helps us to gain greater awareness of this "energy" aspect of ourselves, and it is in part through this awareness that the conscious balancing and integration of energies - or healing - is possible.

Before you begin working with the crystal, take the time to establish contact with the energy flow through your own body. We have been conditioned since birth to isolate and limit our sensing to specific organs of our physical body. We "listen" with our ears, "smell" with our noses etc. This has been part of the process of separateness that contains us within the third Dimension and prevents us from fully integrating with SPIRIT. Divide and conquer ! We need to begin to sense with the wholeness of our being, our bodies, minds and souls as a single, unified being.

Listen to your breath, feel your breath, listen to your heart beat, feel your heart beat. Try to establish how each affects the different parts of your body. Can you feel the energy of your breath flowing down your arms or your legs ? or can you only feel it within your throat and lungs ? Lie quietly for a moment and let yourself experience as deeply as possible the energy flow resulting from both your breath and your heart beat. Are they in harmony ? or are they seemingly in competition ? once you have experienced the flow of each, see if you can merge them together. Try to sense them on a "Wholistic" basis.

Now, having sensed the energy flow within yourself, take your crystal and hold it gently in your hand. Place your attention on the crystal and allow yourself to become aware of its energy. Perhaps it pulses, perhaps it seems to send waves of heat through you. Each of you will experience it differently, there is no right or wrong way to sense. Place it on your brow Chakra, or your Heart Chakra, or on some other part of your body, do you sense its energy any differently ? ask the crystal where it would like to be placed.

Now move your attention back to the flow of energy through your own body, listen again to your breath, feel your heart beat. Have they altered as a result of coming into contact with the energy of the crystal ? You may find that it takes time and practice to attune yourself to your own energy flow sufficiently to detect the difference that a crystal makes, so do not be concerned if it does not seem to happen at this time. Different people respond - or notice that they respond ! - to different amounts of energy, so a small crystal can appear to make a huge difference to the flow of energy in one person, yet not be perceptible to another person. "Know" that there is an interaction of energy, and work with that "Knowing", the sensing will follow eventually, for you will find that sensing is only a confirmation of your existing "Knowing" - the Third Dimensional "Proof" that we all seem to crave !

Becoming energy sensitive and aware is a gradual process, a relaxation and surrender. It involves a letting go of "Doing" and a focusing of your attention inward. Sometimes we are so intent on "making things happen" that we fail to acknowledge that which already "IS". On a physical level, crystal energy interacts with us through a process of resonance, so it is important to become attuned to the flow and the interplay of these energies. Attunement therefore involves coming into at - one - ment with the Crystal energy.

There is so much more I could say about working with Crystals on this new basis, but what is the point, when you can experience it yourself just by opening to the acceptance that all "life" is not made in the image of 'Man'. Hold your crystal in your hand and speak to it as a fellow "Soul" - and more importantly, LISTEN to it as a fellow "Soul" !!.

2

HARMONY OF HEALING THROUGH CRYSTALS PART 2 : THE HEALING PROCESS

"HEALTH REFLECTS YOUR ATTITUDE TO LIFE

FOCUS NOT ON THE ILLNESS YOU WISH TO CURE

FOCUS INSTEAD ON THE WELLNESS YOU WISH TO ACHIEVE"

Once you have established an at - one - ment with your crystals, you can start to look at the process involved in healing through crystals.

With or without the help and assistance of crystals, the healing process involves the healing of **ALL** parties **SIMULTANEOUSLY.** There is no healer or patient, although we invariably use these terms. There is only the **HEALING PROCESS** itself, and that applies equally to all those concerned.

If one thinks that he or she is a "healer", or is attached to being the healer on an ego level, then the situation is created where that person can only be the giver, closing themselves to the possibility of receiving. Such a situation can only be sustained for a short time before the person is drained of energy. In such instances, that person is responsible for disturbing their own energy balance, although all too often they believe they have "picked up stuff" from their "patient". Ensuring that there is a free flow of energy between all parties is therefore most important.

It is also important not to move to the opposite extreme and perceive oneself purely as a channel for healing energy from other (Cosmic or crystal) sources, with no personal input or control. At all times you need to accept responsibility for the energy you are working with, whether this is personal energy, cosmic energy or crystal energy. You have accepted a partnership in the healing process, and with partnership comes responsibility.

In terms of personal healing, the free flow of energy is between you and the crystal. We mentioned in part 1 that such healing can be a "direct" or an "indirect" process. It can involve the placement of the crystal on specific areas of your body or in areas of proximity to your body for a more general effect. In the first instance you are looking at dealing with predetermined "conditions", whereas in the second instance you are looking at the creation of an environment of "wellness" within your life. Even in the situation where there are predetermined "conditions" it is important not to be drawn into the trap of concentrating entirely on the known symptoms and ignoring the deeper causes, which is why it is important to focus always on "Outcomes" - on the state of "wellness" not the state of "illness". If you are drawn to place crystals on specific areas of your body, ask the crystal to connect you, if possible, to the source of the problem, and help you effect a healing on ALL levels, because the physical manifestation of "illness" is the visible end product of disharmony that is occurring in many other layers of your Being.

You can "inspire" a Crystal to hold your "intention" and continue working on the healing while you are engaged in some other activity. Because crystals focus, direct and amplify energy. they will help you to manifest whatever intention you place within them, Once again, however, you are engaged in a mutual process, as when you "inspire" a crystal. the crystal is simultaneously inspiring you to raise your Spiritual awareness, clarity and honesty.

This process of "inspiring" crystals has erroneously become known as programming, but having accepted that you are working with another living, conscious Being, you will realize that what you are doing is forging a contract with a friend to undertake a specific healing task.

Crystals function as a bridge between the Spiritual and the physical realms, and the energy that crystals provide is both physical and spiritual in nature. When you are working with crystals, therefore, you are working with the universal life energy of SPIRIT, and it is important that you are in touch with, and connected to Spirit - particularly your own. To begin to "know" and "understand" the universal life energy of Spirit, you will need to make a quantum leap beyond the five senses into the world of "knowing" rather than "proving". So it is with crystals, for they function at a level that is beyond the five senses.

Before beginning any healing process - on yourself or with someone else - it is important to connect with the Spirit aspect of yourself. "Centre yourself" is often the term used, and it means just what it says, focus on the "centre" of your Being - your Spirit. Once you have done this, you then connect with your Crystal, also on that "Spirit" level. Open the channels of communication between the two "Centres" and allow a state of Harmony and Love to develop between you. When you are sharing a healing with someone else *"ask to be connected to them on a Soul level, to be directed appropriately so that the sharing may be for the highest good of all those participating".* You are now ready to contribute to the healing process.

Perhaps at this point I should remind you that when you are engaged in the healing process with another Being, you are working with three individual, conscious energies. Your own, the crystal's and the patient's. Once again I give you a personal view that you may or may not resonate with. Before becoming engaged in the healing process with another person - **ASK PERMISSION FROM**

THEIR SOUL CENTRE !, something simple along the lines of "Do I have a role to play in this person's healing ?" will suffice. Having been given the go ahead, I then seek to meld my aura with theirs to minimize any disruption to the flow of energy between us. If you use this technique, you need to be conscious of the aura melding at all times and not make any sudden moves that might "tear" the auras apart, and remember to disengage the auras at the completion of the healing process.

Because you are engaging in the healing process at an energy level, the natural starting point is the main energy control points on the physical body, the Chakras. The word "Chakra" means wheel in Sanskrit, and this accurately describes them, as each is a spinning vortex of energy. As the Chakras spin and release energy into the body, these energies saturate the body cells with life and vitality. This energy or vitality then radiates out through the force field (the Aura) that surrounds the body. If the Chakras are not balanced, or if the energies are blocked, the basic life force will be slowed down.

Although there are many Chakras operating throughout the body, it is generally recognized that there are seven major Chakras that need to be in balance and harmony for a feeling of wellbeing to be evident. These Chakras are the Base or Root Chakra, the Sacral Chakra, the Solar Plexus Chakra, the Heart Chakra, the Throat Chakra, the Third Eye Chakra and the Crown Chakra. There are also two other Chakras that some people work on regularly, they are the Spleen Chakra and the Thymus Chakra (the Spleen Chakra is between the Sacral Chakra and the Solar Plexus Chakra and the Thymus Chakra is between the Heart Chakra and the Throat Chakra).

Whether working on yourself or someone else, it is usual to place a crystal on each of the major Chakra points. Once again, talk to your crystals to see which one desires to work with which Chakra, you may find that some crystals always like to work with the same Chakra because they may resonate on the same frequency as it, other crystals will like to vary their placement according to the circumstances of the healing.

There are many differing views and opinions on the healing process involved in working on the Chakras, so it is a situation of accepting that which feels right for you. I can only give you my personal views, they may resonate with you or they may not. I believe that it is not for me to determine whether a particular Chakra should be "open" or "closed", that is the role of the person themselves or their "Higher Soul Self". I may test the energy of a Chakra and find that the flow is weak, and this may indicate that the Chakra is partially closed, however, for me to seek to open that Chakra may cause problems for the person rather than alleviate them. For example, it is quite possible after a death or a trauma that the heart Chakra needs to be partially closed in order for the person to deal with the situation in a balanced way, if I come along and automatically seek to open that Chakra, it may result in such a flood of emotion into the heart that the person will be made worse, not better. I believe that my role in the healing process is to try to ensure that the energy is free flowing through the Chakra at whatever level is appropriate to the person at that time. When working on Chakras I therefore always ask that ***"The energy be free flowing through this Chakra, open or closed as the Higher Soul Self requires"***. As I am asking this I move my hand, or a Crystal wand, in an anti clockwise direction from the body outwards, then in a clockwise direction back in towards the body. This follows the spiral nature of the energy vortex of the Chakra, but the movements themselves - and the direction of them - remains a personal option rather than a "must do" !

When I have done this for all the Chakras, I then seek to ensure that there is a free flow of energy "between" the Chakras - because all are part of the **ONE**. I do this by placing the left hand at the crown Chakra and the right hand at each of the other Chakras in turn and moving them gently in unison one way then the other - much as you would use a pipe cleaner to clean a pipe. I then move on to look at the balance between certain Chakras - usually the third eye with the throat, the heart and the solar plexus. Then the throat with the heart and the solar plexus. Then the heart with the solar plexus. I simply ask that they be "as ONE, in perfect harmony and perfect balance ".

While you are working with the crystals on this general energy balance and empowerment, you may be made aware of an energy blockage, or you may have been pre warned by the patient of a particular area that feels disharmonious, so when the general balance is over, some or all of the crystals can be moved to the area of discomfort or imbalance and placed in a circle, a square or a cross over the area. Be guided by your own intuition and by what the crystals are conveying to you. Do not assume that the crystals will "know" your intention in changing the emphasis of the healing process from a general balance to a specific problem solving, speak to them, ask them to tune in to the problem just as you are tuning in to the problem. It is fair to say that the whole healing process should be a continual dialogue between you, the crystals and the person you are working with, on a Soul or Spirit level (much as a team of doctors involved in an operation are in constant communication with each other).

The other question that presents itself at the commencement of the healing process - or, indeed, at some point within it - is, what type of crystals should one be working with ? Some crystal workers are more comfortable working with clear quartz, others with crystals that more closely match the colour vibrations of the particular Chakras. There is no right or wrong in this matter, only personal preference - and, of course, advice from your crystal partners ! The more you become hooked on "Do's" and Don'ts" the less spontaneous you become, and therefore the less in tune with the flow and interchange of dynamic energies that represent the healing process. I often begin with the clear quartz for the general balance then move to other crystals on certain Chakras if that's what seems needed. Even then, the crystal that calls out to work with a certain Chakra may not seem the most appropriate one (from the information you have been given in books or by other Crystal workers) - Rose Quartz on the third eye, for example.

Many people seek out specific crystals for personal or inter-personal healing based on information gathered from the many crystal books available at this time, and there is nothing wrong with that as a starting point ! however, most books generalise on a "species" basis because they are not written from a standpoint of the Conscious, Living aspect of crystals. To say, for example, that all Citrines "balance emotions and makes the mood sunny and cheerful" is a bit like saying that "all Welsh people are great singers" - there is an element of truth or anecdotal evidence to support the claim, but it is a definite generalization !! It would also be fair to say that a lot of the "healing powers" attributed to specific crystals relate as much to their "colour" vibrational affinity with a Chakra or body organ as to their individual crystalline structure. The rule of thumb, therefore, continues to be, **LOOK,**

LISTEN, THEN MAKE UP YOUR OWN MIND !!, and at all times COMMUNICATE WITH THE INDIVIDUAL CRYSTAL !!

"Thought" projection is an important part of the healing process. It creates the necessary flow of energy between you, the crystal and the person you are sharing the healing with. It is important therefore that your thoughts at all times are "outcome" directed. In other words do not allow your thoughts to dwell on the negative aspects of the "illness" or "disease", but on the positive aspects of "wellbeing" and a "state of harmony and perfection". Also, do not get hung up on "seeing", "sensing" or "picking up information" during a healing session, as this creates blockages in the flow of energy. Trying too hard to be "sensitive" invariably results in frustration, and this is hardly helpful to the healing process that you are sharing. Unfortunately. many of those you will be sharing the healing process with are themselves hung up on the theatrics of "sensing", and expect some miraculous diagnosis from it. **Do not let this concern you.** Work with all the energies at your disposal in a positive life affirming way, and "know" that what you are sharing is beneficial to all parties involved. Any thing else that you "pick up" during the healing process should be regarded as a bonus rather than a necessity.

Perhaps, when you are gathering together the crystals that will be working with you in your partnership of healing, you should ask to have a crystal to assist in the area of "sensing" as well as healing. By putting out this thought it is quite likely that such a crystal will come to you. That crystal could be placed near to the body, or even on the body at various places during the healing session, to monitor, amplify and draw to your conscious attention any information that could be important to the mental as well as physical wellbeing of the other party in the healing process. But the basic message to remember is, simply let the healing energies flow, and accept the joys implicit within the sharing itself.

ALL HEALING SHOULD BE A JOY FILLED INTERACTION OF ENERGY.

3

AMAZONITE

Greetings

I am SPIRIT

SPIRIT of Crystals and Gemstones

I come before you in true Light and Infinite Love to share and guide your exploration of the wondrous beauty of my Earthly Children, the Crystals.

Each Crystal is a unique vibration, and each has its own Guardian to direct its work in the Earth Dimension, but all Crystals are ONE with SPIRIT.

I ask you now to relax and place your attention on the Crystal you hold in your left hand.

Focus on your breathing. Breathe in, hold, breathe out. Breathe in, hold, breathe out. As you breathe

in, imagine that your whole Being is enveloped in a pale green shimmering Light, as you breathe in, absorb the essence of the healing green. As you breathe out, feel the mists that have veiled your eyes lifting and dispersing. Breathe in the shimmering green Light, breathe out the veiling mists.

Feel yourself opening and awakening to the Spiritual bounty that life has to offer. You have now joined the vibration of the Amazonite.

My child the Amazonite works to strengthen all the energy currents within the body, but it has an especially powerful effect on aligning both the Heart and Solar Plexus Chakras, and the Etheric and mental bodies. This is important both for healing and for Spiritual growth, for it allows people to develop more fully their inner vision, and to communicate that vision with honesty and integrity in all situations. Indeed, in times past my child the Amazonite has been considered the "Seer's Stone", unlocking the "Starlight vision" and giving its wearer the ability to see the past, present, and future with depth and clarity. Its impeccable energy promotes candour, openness, truth and trust, encouraging people to speak from the Heart with total honesty.

Now, relax completely. Raise your left hand and place your Crystal at a point between your Solar Plexus and your Heart. Feel the two Chakras open and expand until they become as ONE HARMONIOUS VIBRATION. Now, move the Crystal slowly up your body until it rests comfortably over your third Eye. You have created a channel between your inner emotions and your inner vision, which will allow you to see all aspects of your total Cosmic Being.

Feel the green vibration of the Amazonite opening your own "Starlight vision", allowing you to raise to your conscious mind the whole panorama of your past lives in this Dimension, and in other Dimensions. It will be as if you are watching an epic film, with no personal emotional involvement or reaction. My child will allow you to observe without fear and without judgement. Observe now the panorama of your past.

As you let your past lives fade from your conscious mind, wrap them in the healing mantle of Universal Love and thank them for the growth they have brought you. Next, allow your present lifetime to be raised to the screen of your conscious mind, and watch it unfold without fear and without judgement. View it with honesty, seeing and accepting all of its many colours, and degrees of Light. As your present also fades from view, send it the healing rays of Universal Love, and give it thanks for the growth and wisdom that it has brought you.

You may ask now for some visions of the future to be raised on to the screen of your mind, view it once more without fear or judgement, accepting that what you see is possibility, not certainty, for the choices that you as an individual and you as a collective Earth Consciousness make will create, and possibly transform, the canvass that my child the Amazonite is helping you to perceive at this moment. Enjoy for a moment your visions of tomorrow. As the images of tomorrow fade into the distance, send them the healing vibration of Universal Love, and give thanks for the growth and the wisdom that is yet to fill your conscious life with its joyful vibration.

Slowly draw your Crystal down from your third Eye to that point between your Heart Chakra and your Solar Plexus Chakra, bringing your consciousness gently back into your physical body.

Focus once more on your Breathing. Breathe in, hold, breathe out. Breathe in, hold breathe out. As you breathe out, fill your aura with the vibration of truth and Light and allow that vibration to reach out and touch each person you meet, each situation you encounter, each and every aspect of your Joy filled life.

All are now ONE with my child the Amazonite.

I am SPIRIT.

SPIRIT of Crystals and Gemstones.

Blessings be upon you.

4

AMETHYST

Greetings

I am SPIRIT

SPIRIT of Crystals and Gemstones

I come before you in true Light and Infinite Love to share and guide your exploration of the wondrous beauty of my Earthly Children, the Crystals.

Each Crystal is a unique vibration, and each has its own Guardian to direct its work in the Earth Dimension, but all Crystals are ONE with SPIRIT.

I ask you now to relax and place your attention on the Crystal you hold in your left hand.

Focus on your breathing, breathe in, hold, breathe out. Breathe in, hold, breathe out. As you breathe

in, imagine you are filling your body with a mist of vibrant purple. As you breathe out, imagine all the blockages and imbalances melting from your body. Breathe in the purple mist, breathe out the blockages and imbalances.

Feel a new sense of equilibrium flow through your physical and emotional Being as you become ONE with the purple mist. You have now joined the vibration of the Amethyst.

Amethyst is a true child of SPIRIT. It is the designated carrier of the purple Ray, and this Ray draws ones attention towards SPIRIT. The Crystal that carries this Ray must do everything possible to assist its wearers to focus their attention on SPIRIT. For this reason, Amethyst has a strong balancing effect upon and between ones emotions, memory, mind, subconscious, and the physical body. When these are balanced and aligned, a greater flow of SPIRIT force can flow into the physical body. SPIRIT force is also the life force and the healing force.

The purple Ray, with the Amethyst vibratory rate behind it, opens the circuit of energy flowing through the throat Chakra and out through the brow Chakra. When this occurs people become able to see into their inner worlds. This in turn brings SPIRITUAL unfoldment.

Let us experience this together. Take your Amethyst in your left hand and raise it to the area of your throat Chakra, and let it rest there. Ask for the energy of the purple Ray, and the vibration of the Amethyst to flow into your Being. Allow your consciousness to float on that liquid stream of energy deeper and deeper into your Soul Dimension. Feel the calmness that envelops you. Feel the ropes of fear that bind you to past attitudes melt away. Feel the gentle light bathe and heal you. The deeper you move, the brighter becomes the Light, for the purple Ray seeks out and dismantles the shadows that have accumulated over your many lifetimes.

You step from those shadows into a space of infinite beauty, an oasis of Peace and Harmony. There are others within that space, Beings of your Dimension and Beings of other Dimensions, reach out to them, embrace them with your Love. Have you ever imagined such serenity? such a feeling of completeness? Savour it, absorb it, for you will take the essence of it with you when you return to your Earth Dimension. Look around you, perhaps you see your Guide, perhaps you see a long forgotten friend, call out to them in Joy, recognize that they are a part of all that you have become.

This tranquil place is both a retreat and a meeting place. You can choose to enjoy its radiant beauty in solitude, or you can choose to share it with companion Souls from other Dimensions. Either way you will find no discord or disharmony in its embrace, for this is the space of perfect balance within yourself. My child the Amethyst will help you to connect to this space at any time, and draw the benefits of its balanced energies back in to your day to day life, for in balance lies healing of infinite power.

For the moment, however, relax and enjoy the solitude or the company, whichever is your choice for tonight.

Once more it is time to begin the return journey to your conscious Earth Dimension, but remember this, the core of your Being is the source and fountainhead of the greatest wisdom that can ever be known. The Amethyst, like all my other Crystal children, do not provide the wisdom for you, they simply provide a vehicle to help you to look inward to the core of your Being and recognize the truth of what you see.

Now, allow yourself to flow gently back along the ribbon of purple, bringing with you some of the tranquillity that you experienced in your inner space. Feel yourself re-connecting with your physical body, and as you do, feel all the elements of disharmony being displaced from your physical Being. Anger, fear, hatred, all melting away.

Focus once more on your breathing. Breathe in, hold, breathe out. Breathe in, hold, breathe out. Now, as you breathe out, allow the new found balance and Harmony to radiate from your Being to embrace the Planet on which you live, for the Earth also needs to be touched by the healing energies of Peace, Love and Harmony.

All are now ONE with my child the Amethyst.

I am SPIRIT.

SPIRIT of Crystals and Gemstones.

Blessings be upon you.

5

AQUAMARINE

Greetings

I am SPIRIT

SPIRIT of Crystals and Gemstones

I come before you in true Light and Infinite Love to share and guide your exploration of the wondrous beauty of my Earthly Children, the Crystals.

Each Crystal is a unique vibration, and each has its own Guardian to direct its work in the Earth Dimension, but all Crystals are ONE with SPIRIT.

I ask you now to relax and place your attention on the Crystal you hold in your left hand.

Focus on your breathing, breathe in, hold, breathe out. Breathe in, hold, breathe out. As you breathe

in, feel the soothing blue/green waves wash through your body. As you breathe out, feel your Spiritual inhibitions ebb away like flotsam on the receding tide. Breathe in the blue/green wave, breathe out the Spiritual inhibitions.

Feel yourself becoming a part of the inner ocean, that vast area of liquidity. knowledge and wisdom within each individual. You have now joined the vibration of Aquamarine.

Allow the gentle essence of the Aquamarine to seep into every pore of your Being until you become ONE with the nurturing oceans of the Universe. Imagine yourself transported on a wisp of blue/green cloud to the shores of a tropical lagoon. Sit on the sun kissed sand and gaze into the clear depths of the shimmering water. Call softly to your friends the Dolphins, reach out to them in Love and they will come to guide you on your journey.

Have no fear, step slowly but purposefully into the water, allow the Dolphin to approach you and tune in to your vibration of Love and Light. When she is satisfied that you are ready to undertake your journey, she will take you by the hand and lead you deeper and deeper into the Ocean's depths. Go with her Joyfully. Strangely, as you go deeper it does not become darker, the Light seems to hover around you, to move with you, as if it is a part of you.

The Dolphin leads you to an opening in the majestic coral, and guides you inside, to a subterranean world of incredible beauty. Before you towers a Palace of Ice Blue Crystal, and you gaze upon it with silent awe, wondering who could possibly have created such a sculpture of perfection. You feel drawn to it, even though it has an air of emptiness about it, and you turn to ask the Dolphin for an explanation, but the Dolphin is no longer there, she has been transmuted by the magic of the Ice Blue Crystal into your own Guide or Guardian Angel.

They smile, and beckon you to enter the Crystal Together you step through the archway and look around, and immediately the Light you have brought with you causes the Crystal to glow and vibrate with a new vital energy. Inside you find a complex structure of many levels, each level containing many rooms, and you are puzzled. Then the realization comes that you are seeing the deeper aspects of your own multi-Dimensional Being. You are being invited by my child the Aquamarine to open the doors to your inner Ocean and Light up more and more of the areas within it. Some will pull back, unwilling or unable yet to face the truth within themselves, others will move from room to room filling them with Light and Sound, to increase awareness and comprehension of who they are and what their purpose and potentials may be for this lifetime.

It is up to you how much or how little you explore and en-Lighten your Palace of Ice Blue Crystal. Walk in the protection of your Guide or Guardian Angel.

The time is all too short in this enchanted place, and once more you are drawn to the edge of the water. Your Guide bids you farewell, and once more transmutes into the Joyful Dolphin, who takes you gently by the hand and guides you on your return journey to the golden sand of your lagoon. Rest a moment as you take stock of what has occurred, know that you can return at any time to further increase the areas of en-Lightenment and awareness within yourself, simply by sharing once more with my child the Aquamarine. Before you leave, send healing Love to your friend and guide, the Dolphin, visualize her spreading that healing Love to all the other creatures of the sea, and to all the oceans of the World. Embrace your ONENESS with the whole Marine environment.

Now, allow yourself to float gently back on your blue/green cloud to permeate once again the Physical aspect of your Being. Bring with you the new awareness that you have created with your en-Lightenment of your inner oceans.

Focus once more on your breathing. Breathe in, hold, breathe out, Breathe in, hold, breathe out. As you breathe out, allow your new en-Lightenment to dispel the shadows of doubt and uncertainty that have held you back on your journey of growth. Light your path with the radiant vibration of my child the Aquamarine.

I am SPIRIT.

SPIRIT of Crystals and Gemstones.

Blessings be upon you.

6

AVENTURINE

Greetings

I am SPIRIT

SPIRIT of Crystals and Gemstones

I come before you in true Light and Infinite Love to share and guide your exploration of the wondrous beauty of my Earthly Children, the Crystals.

Each Crystal is a unique vibration, and each has its own guardian to direct its work in the Earth Dimension, but all Crystals are ONE with SPIRIT.

I ask you now to relax and place your attention on the Crystal you hold in your left hand.

Focus on your breathing, breathe in, hold, breathe out. Breathe in, hold, breathe out. As you breathe

in. fill your aura with the deep, deep green of the tropical Rainforest. As you breathe out, imagine all disharmony and disease being expelled from your body. Breathe in the deep, deep green, breathe out the disharmony.

Feel your whole body pulsate with a new, dynamic, healing frequency. You have now joined the vibration of the Aventurine.

If you look at the Earth Planet with the eye of knowingness, you will see that everywhere people are ready for an awakening of Spirituality, a new Enlightenment. But all too often their attention, and therefore their energies, are distracted by the disease and disharmony within the physical body. My child the Aventurine seeks to create healing within the physical so that a greater focus can be placed on this Spiritual awakening. Working essentially on the major organs of the body, it aligns with, and amplifies, the healthy vibrations of the organ to gradually expel any vibrations of disharmony or disease. At times the body itself needs assistance to dispose of the toxins expelled by the actions of the Aventurine within the organs, so it often works best in conjunction with the primary carrier of the Healing Green Ray, my child the Emerald.

By working to remove the distractions created within the physical, the Aventurine allows you to see more clearly the potentials and alternatives in the mundane, practical side of life, and on a higher level, when you see many alternatives, it becomes easier to tap into your own unique creative flow. So even though it deals essentially with physical healing, Aventurine serves to create a free flowing energy for Spiritual Enlightenment.

Place your Crystal over your Heart Chakra and draw the healing vibration of the Aventurine deep into the centre of your Being. Imagine yourself walking slowly down a path of dark mottled green, the sun occasionally sending shafts of silvery Light down through the canopy high overhead, seeming to capture, as if in a spotlight, the vibrant colours of the Rainforest Flowers. Enjoy the beauty and unique balance of this special environment, for within it lies healing of immense, untapped, power. The path winds onwards until it reaches a Rainbow drenched clearing, where the sun struggles to penetrate the misty spray of a mighty waterfall.

Move forward into the Rainbow spray, feel it cleansing you as it lightly caresses your skin, feel your Chakras vibrate to the colours of the Rainbow as they flow deep within your Being. Feel your emotions begin to find a new balance. Now, move back to the edge of the Rainforest and absorb the healing power of its deep green vibration. Perhaps there is a plant or a tropical flower that draws you closer to share a special healing vibration that you need, embrace it with Love. From the decay littered floor of the Rainforest majestic trees reach upwards to embrace the Light, absorbing its life giving energies then channeling that energy back to the nurturing mantle of the earth. But this can only happen if the physical body of the tree is healthy and balanced. This is also true in your life and your Dimension.

You can always return to this healing waterfall within the Rainforest, for its vibration is within my child the Aventurine. But for now it is time to retrace your steps along the mottled green path, through the patches of silver sunshine, back into your physical body. Feel your energy concentrate in your Heart Chakra, then move slowly outwards to fill your Aura with healing Green Light.

Focus once more on your breathing, breathe in, hold, breathe out, Breathe in, hold breath out. As you breath out, allow the healing Green light to connect you with Rainforests all over the world. Embrace them with your Love, care for them, nurture them, forge a special relationship with their unique healing energies.

Now you are ONE with my child the Aventurine.

I am SPIRIT

SPIRIT of Crystals and Gemstones

Blessings be upon you.

7

BLUE LACE AGATE

Greetings

I am **SPIRIT**

SPIRIT OF CRYSTALS AND GEMSTONES

I come before you in true Light and infinite Love to share and guide your exploration of the wondrous beauty of my Earthly Children, the Crystals.

Each Crystal is a unique vibration, and each has its own guardian to direct its work within the Earth Dimension, but all Crystals are **ONE** with **SPIRIT.**

I ask you now to relax and place your attention on the Crystal you hold in your left hand.

Focus on your breathing. Breathe in, hold, breathe out. Breathe in, hold, breathe out. As you breathe

in, imagine yourself being embraced by a gentle light blue mist, draw it slowly into the very depths of your Being. As you breathe out, feel the tentacles of stress and anger unwinding and lifting from your body. Breathe in the gentle light blue mist, breathe out the tentacles of stress and anger.

Feel yourself melting slowly into the Dimension of tranquillity and serenity. You have now joined the vibration of the Blue Lace Agate.

On both a physical and an emotional level, my child the Blue Lace Agate works to cool the overheated state. It neutralizes the "Hot" energies of inflammation, fever and infection on a physical level, and cools anger, hot tempers and stress on an emotional level. It is therefore an important tool in both healing and meditation. As it draws you into the realms of calmness and coolness it helps you to open and expand, enhancing creativity and confidence. Its gentle blue bathes the throat Chakra with healing light to encourage your communication skills, allowing you to explore and express more openly your inner wisdom. The wisdom of **PEACE**. For when you find peace within yourself, you begin to radiate that peace to others. This is at the heart of the work that my child the Blue Lace Agate performs within your Dimension, it is the **DOVE OF PEACE** from the Crystal Dimension, creating from the fires of the physical, the serenity of the Soul.

Now, allow yourself to relax completely, lift the Blue Lace Agate to rest gently on your throat Chakra. Feel the pulse in your throat become **ONE** with the Crystal as your Heart embraces its tranquility. Feel the last embers of tension flow from your body. Imagine you have become weightless, floating gently on a magic carpet of blue. The carpet becomes your inter Dimensional transporter, moving you swiftly from your Earth Dimension to a distant Planet. A Planet where only **PEACE** and **LOVE** exist, wrapped in an atmosphere of serene blue.

This was once a Planet just like yours, filled with turmoil, anger, fear, hatred and war, until the Guardians came with their gift of Blue Light, and offered an alternative to the total destruction that seemed such an inevitable consequence. Sit for a while and allow the essence of what this Planet has achieved to flow through every fibre of your Being. Feel the incredible depth of its serenity. It's a vibration unlike any you have experienced before. **TOTAL LOVE. TOTAL PEACE, TOTAL SERENITY**. Become **ONE** with that vibration.

Peace within the individual begins at the centre of the Heart and flows outwards on waves of **LOVE**, until every aspect of the Being is alight with its vibration, but for a whole Planet to become **ONE** with **PEACE** requires the communication of that vibration one Being to another. The empowerment of the Throat Chakra is central to that process, for it is not sufficient to FEEL peace within one's self, one must express it openly and honestly for it to become the dominant reality of existence. Take this truth with you as you return on your magic carpet of Blue Light, to your own Planet and your own Dimension.

Focus once more on your breathing. Breathe in, hold, breathe out. Breathe in, hold, breathe out. As you breathe out, send the vibrations of **PEACE** and **SERENITY** out into the room you are in, out into the world you are in, out into the Universe you are in.

All are now **ONE** with my child the **BLUE LACE AGATE**

I am **SPIRIT**

SPIRIT OF CRYSTALS AND GEMSTONES

Blessings be upon you

8

CARNELIAN

Greetings

I am SPIRIT

SPIRIT of Crystals and Gemstones

I come before you in true Light and Infinite Love to share and guide your exploration of the wondrous beauty of my Earthly Children, the Crystals.

Each Crystal is a unique vibration, and each has its own Guardian to direct its work in the Earth Dimension, but all Crystals are ONE with SPIRIT.

I ask you now to relax and place your attention on the Crystal you hold in your left hand.

Focus on your breathing, breathe in, hold, breathe out. Breathe in, hold, breathe out. As you breathe

in, imagine your body being filled with the gentle orange of an Australian Sunset. As you breathe out, imagine all unnecessary clutter within your mind clearing away. Breathe in the gentle orange sunset, breathe out the unnecessary clutter.

Feel yourself becoming clearer and lighter as the gentle orange attunes you to the simple rhythm of Mother Earth. You have now joined the vibration of the Carnelian.

Most of my children have colour within them, but few are given the extra responsibility of carrying one of the seven primary colour Rays. Carnelian has such a responsibility in bringing to the Earth Planet the life giving energy of the Orange Ray. This is the Ray that teaches the balance between the positive, negative and neutralizing forces in life, relaxing the emotions and creating a calmer, more balanced existence.

But Carnelian is more than simply a carrier of the Orange Ray. Its Crystal vibration is closely attuned to the eternal cycle of Earth seasons, reminding that life does not end, but circles endlessly. No fear of death in Carnelian's embrace, for it will allow you to share past lives and past experiences in order to pave the way for the new. This enables you to take control of your life, and choose the direction that is most advantageous to you.

Embrace now the mellow vibration of the Carnelian. Allow it to transport you to a mystical valley slumbering peacefully between towering mist covered peaks. Through the valley runs a swift. clear stream, darting over and around the rocks that seek to block its path. Sit for a moment and watch the joyous dance of the sparkling water, see how it catches the burnished hue of the early morning sun flickering through the rising valley mists. It becomes a stream of liquid fire, cleansing the soil over which it passes, moving aside the debris of the past, refusing to allow pools of stagnant water to form, moving, always moving, as if filled with infinite curiosity.

Dip your hand into the cool crystal water, feel its strength of purpose, feel that same energy rising into your body. Flushing away the dead and dirty autumn leaves of your past, filling you with a new sense of anticipation and excitement about the future. Now, look around you at the trees of burnished gold, see how they too shed their autumn leaves, knowing full well that in so doing they prepare not for death, but for a new life. Allow yourself to become a part of that natural cycle of nature, be ONE with the stream and the trees, recognizing the eternal quality of your own existence.

Neither the stream or the trees seek to erase the past, they honour it as a foundation for their future, and they build on it. My child the Carnelian will help you to do likewise.

Autumn is the time of harvest, the time when the seeds of spring have ripened to their full potential. As you sit amidst this tranquil autumn splendor, think about the plans, dreams and ideas that you have sown during your many lifetimes, which of these is ready to be harvested ? which of these do you now WISH to harvest ?. Take the Carnelian and lift it to your third Eye, imagine, visualize or simply wish for the manifestation of that special dream that you have been working hard to nurture and create in your life. Ask the Carnelian energy to help you harvest that dream. Believe that you are worthy of it !

Take a final look around your mystical valley, at the dappled orange and yellow hues of the autumn trees, at the joyous, babbling stream of molten gold that links the past and the future, and feel in those things the fabric of your own existence. Now, bid them farewell, and move gently back into your own physical Dimension.

Focus once more on your breathing. Breathe in, hold, breathe out. Breathe in, hold, breathe out. Now, as you breathe out, feel your own connection with Mother Earth becoming stronger and more Loving. Feel your breath becoming ONE with the rhythm of the environment.

Embrace and enjoy my child the Carnelian.

I am SPIRIT.

SPIRIT of Crystals and Gemstones.

Blessings be upon you.

9

CITRINE

Greetings

I am SPIRIT

SPIRIT of Crystals and Gemstones

I come before you in true Light and Infinite Love to share and guide your exploration of the wondrous beauty of my Earthly Children, the Crystals.

Each Crystal is a unique vibration, and each has its own Guardian to direct its work in the Earth Dimension, but all Crystals are ONE with SPIRIT.

I ask you now to relax and place your attention on the Crystal you hold in your left hand.

Focus on your breathing. Breathe in, hold, breathe out. Breathe in, hold, breathe out. As you breathe in,

imagine the golden yellow of the sunlight flooding your aura, Lighting your whole Being. As you breathe out, imagine all the disharmonies unwinding from your Chakras. Breathe in the golden yellow sunshine, breathe out the disharmonies.

Feel the flow of energies through your Being move into proper natural alignment. You have now joined the vibration of the Citrine.

Sound is equally as important to life as Light is, but the sound is often difficult to hear among the noises of daily living. This is a great sadness to me, for each Crystal carries its own music, which is unique and enchantingly beautiful. If people are able to hear, or imagine that they hear, the Sound of a Crystal when they wear it, its power will be magnified dramatically. This is because the wearer will become more in tune with that Crystal's vibratory rate. My child the Citrine will help people to become more familiar with the Sound of the life force energy, because it carries its aspect of the yellow colour Ray more in its Sound than in its Light.

Take a moment to place the Citrine to your ear, and listen to its joyful melody.

Citrine is not the official carrier of the yellow Ray. That Crystal is yet to emerge and blossom as the Planet and its people draw closer in their evolution to accepting the full power of the yellow Ray. Citrine prepares all aspects of an individual to receive a greater amount of the yellow Ray, then acts as a magnet to draw this yellow Ray to it. Although the yellow Ray is one of the seven colour Rays that splits from the pure white Light of SPIRIT, it is the only colour that reflects the realms of God and the Source of all life.

My child the Citrine opens you to the awareness that your Earthly plane and your Earthly bodies are gifts from the Creator, gifts to be cherished and enjoyed. Allow yourself to be transported on its beam of golden yellow sunlight to the pristine sands of your personal Island Paradise, feel the warmth and Love of the sun bathing you in its life giving glow. Look around you at the infinite bounty that the energy of the Sun has provided, but more importantly, LISTEN. Listen to the gentle hum of life itself. to the lilting warble of the birds in flight and the birds nesting in the lush tropical foliage. Listen to the soft caress of the waves as they cool the sun drenched Crystals of sand beneath your feet, to the splash of Dolphins playing joyfully in the surf. Listen to the breath of Heaven in the voice of the gentle breeze. But most of all, Listen to the Heartbeat of SPIRIT within YOURSELf.

Truth and wisdom radiate forth from the Heartbeat of SPIRIT within you like radio waves through the many Galaxies of the Universe. Tune into them, allow my child the Citrine to enhance the clarity of your listening.

But now it is time once more to leave your Paradise Island and return on your golden yellow beam of sunlight to the consciousness of your physical Dimension, bringing with you a new clarity of Spiritual sight and Spiritual Hearing.

Focus once more on your breathing. Breathe in, hold, breathe out. Breathe in, hold, breathe out. As you breathe out, allow the sunshine you have absorbed in your travels to pour forth, Lightening, brightening and warming your whole environment.

All is now in the joyful, energizing embrace of my child the Citrine.

I am SPIRIT.

SPIRIT of Crystals and Gemstones.

Blessings be upon you.

10

HAWK'S EYE

Greetings

I am SPIRIT

SPIRIT of Crystals and Gemstones

I come before you in true Light and Infinite Love to share and guide your exploration of the wondrous beauty of my Earthly Children, the Crystals.

Each Crystal is a unique vibration, and each has its own guardian to direct its work in the Earth Dimension, but all Crystals are ONE with SPIRIT.

I ask you now to relax and place your attention on the Crystal you hold in your left hand.

Focus on your breathing, breathe in, hold, breathe out. Breathe in, hold, breathe out. As you breathe in, feel the deep azure blue of the midnight sky filling your aura and your physical body to capacity. As you breathe out, feel any limiting aspects of your Being lifting and floating away. Breathe in the deep azure blue, breathe out all limiting aspects.

Feel a sense of Peace and serenity suffuse your entire Being. You have now joined the vibration of the Hawk's Eye.

My child the Hawk's Eye is a Crystal of perspective, drawing to you the capacity to view the WHOLENESS of life. Enabling you to see both the Light and the dark aspects of life in your Dimension in a calm, discerning way. Perspective is an alternative to detachment. When you are able to see things as part of the greater whole much of the emotional distortion and confusion is erased. You do not cease to care, as the word detachment sometimes seems to infer, you simply become more aware of the broader picture. This helps you to obtain a greater understanding of how all things ultimately work together for the greatest good.

Once you have a greater perception of the WHOLE, you see more clearly the true bounty of your existence. Problems that seemed insurmountable become as a single grain of sand on a magnificent sweeping beach. As your understanding of the vast panorama of your existence grows, so does your appreciation of it. You begin to discover beauty in all aspects of your life, you begin to feel a greater ONENESS with your environment. My child the Hawk's Eye will lead you back to the nurturing embrace of your Earth Mother, revealing her abundance and her magnificence and creating a new Joy within your life.

Allow yourself to relax completely. Imagine circles of iridescent blue moving from your toes to your head, soothing, nurturing, creating around you a cocoon of vibrant Light. Feel yourself being drawn upwards into the deep blue of the night sky. Find yourself gently transported to a Plateau, high on a craggy snow laden mountain. From this point you can see the World laid out at your feet.

This is the Plateau of Perspective.

Sit for a while and gaze out over your World and over your life, see how each part interlocks, how each contributes to the WHOLE. That mountain that yesterday seemed to block your path can now be seen as a ridge leading to a lush green valley, so when you return to continue your day to day existence, you will look upon your mountain with new understanding. Perspective creates greater freedom in your life. Look at your past and look at your future from the Plateau of Perspective, see what new joys you can discover in the wholeness of your existence.

When life, or some aspect of life, seems to be getting on top of you, return to this Plateau with my child the Hawk's Eye, and view that aspect of your life in Perspective, in its relationship to the WHOLE.

Now, however, it is time to return to your physical Dimension. Allow the circles of iridescent blue to move you gently down from the Plateau, and into your Earthly body.

Focus once more on your breathing. Breathe in, hold breath out. Breathe in, hold breathe out. As you breathe out, fill your aura with the Blue light of understanding and awareness, that you might appreciate the true abundance of your WHOLE existence.

All are now ONE with my child the Hawk's Eye.

I am SPIRIT,

SPIRIT of Crystals and Gemstones.

Blessings be upon you.

11

HEMATITE

Greetings

I am SPIRIT

SPIRIT of Crystals and Gemstones

I come before you in true Light and Infinite Love to share and guide your exploration of the wondrous beauty of my Earthly Children, the Crystals.

Each Crystal is a unique vibration, and each has its own Guardian to direct its work in the Earth Dimension, but all Crystals are ONE with SPIRIT.

I ask you now to relax and place your attention on the Crystal you hold in your left hand.

Focus on your breathing. Breathe in, hold, breathe out. Breathe in, hold, breathe out. Imagine yourself surrounded by a shimmering silver cloud. As you breathe in, feel the shimmering cloud being drawn deep into the essence of your Being. As you breathe out, imagine all the unhealthy toxins being expelled from your body. Breathe in the shimmering silver cloud, breathe out the unhealthy toxins.

Feel yourself becoming more balanced and grounded. You have now joined the vibration of Hematite.

My child the Hematite is a Crystal of knowledge and learning, imparting its wisdom to all who seek to look beyond the surface of life to its deeper, inner meaning. It will encourage you to isolate and use wisely that which is important in any situation, separating the wheat from the chaff. It also teaches you to focus and concentrate energy in a creative way, drawing together the strengths and talents of other people into a cohesive force. As such, my child is an ideal Crystal to assist those working on group projects.

Because the Hematite connects to the earth, it accentuates all the positive aspects of the Earth's energies, creating a solid foundation of strength, stability and reliability, yet at the same time, through its ability to promote clarity of vision, it can provide an energizing influence on any situation, to ensure that stagnation is avoided.

Allow your body and mind to relax completely. Feel yourself being enveloped by the silver cloud of the Hematite. You feel totally safe, totally secure. Imagine yourself floating gently down a winding road. On either side, tall silver birches sway in the breeze, you feel that you can reach out and caress them as you pass, you feel a special ONENESS with them. They guide you to the mouth of a large cave, and you float inside. The walls glisten and shimmer with silver strands, and the floor and ceiling seem to pulsate with a myriad of Crystals. You move deeper and deeper, yet you have no sense of being contained or enclosed. You feel instead a growing sensation of freedom, as if you are being released from all the mundane concerns of your daily life.

You reach a majestic cavern, and your cloud comes slowly to a halt, then evaporates, leaving you standing in a Cathedral of towering Crystals. You look around at the awesome beauty. It seems to radiate Light that is at once powerful, yet infinitely soft. It embraces you with nurturing Love, and you realize that you have been brought to the Heart of the

Earth, to the living essence of the Earth Mother. Sit for a while and enjoy her healing, Loving, energies. Draw strength from her softness. Draw gentleness from her strength. You are not alone, all around you others sit in silent contemplation, rekindling their energies, rediscovering their connection with the inner Soul of your Dimension. Allow yourself to do the same.

Time is all too short in this space of infinite tranquility, and the silver cloud materializes once more, surrounding you and lifting you gently up into its embrace. You gaze once more on the infinite beauty of this Crystal Cathedral, drawing its image deep within your subconscious so you may access it when next you need to find the Peace within yourself. Then, slowly, your silver cloud moves back down the glittering passage, along the road of silver birches, and back into your physical Dimension.

Focus once more on your breathing. Breathe in, hold, breathe out. Breathe in, hold breathe out. As you breathe out, imagine your silver cloud spreading across the globe, bringing Light and Love to all it embraces.

All are now ONE with my child the Hematite.

I am SPIRIT.

SPIRIT of Crystals and Gemstones.

Blessings be upon you.

12

KYANITE

Greetings

I am SPIRIT

SPIRIT of Crystals and Gemstones

I come before you in true Light and Infinite Love to share and guide your exploration of the wondrous beauty of my Earthly Children, the Crystals.

Each Crystal is a unique vibration, and each has its own guardian to direct its work in the Earth Dimension, but all Crystals are ONE with SPIRIT.

I ask you now to relax and place your attention on the Crystal you hold in your left hand.

Focus on your breathing, breathe in, hold, breathe out. Breathe in, hold, breathe out. As you breathe in, feel your aura being filled with the pale blue essence of a clear winter sky. As you breathe out, imagine all your negative thought patterns being gently transformed into Light. Breathe in the pale blue essence, breathe out all negative thought patterns.

Feel the molecular structure of your whole body being gently elevated. You have now joined the vibration of the Kyanite.

You will find in the arms of my child the Kyanite a deep sense of serenity that transports you beyond the realms of your Earthly concerns. By creating an inner calmness and tranquility, it allows you to view your life with greater clarity and understanding, and by transforming the negative thought patterns that bind you to your Earth bound existence, it allows you to access the higher realms of Spiritual awareness with greater ease, both on a conscious and a subconscious level.

My child the Kyanite opens the crown Chakra to facilitate contact and communication with your own Higher Self, and through the vehicle of your Higher Self, opens the way for Astral and Inter-Dimensional travel. The subtle vibration of its translucent pale blue colour, in partnership with its powerful Crystal life force energy, creates a special Dimension for Spiritual Healing, a Dimension that has yet to be fully recognized and utilized on your Earth Planet. Many are awakening to the wondrous benefits of both Earth based energies and Cosmic energies in the healing process, but few are opening their Hearts and minds to the energy vibration of true SPIRIT. My child the Kyanite opens the door to this process of healing through SPIRIT essence, by creating the bridge to that special Dimension.

Now, raise your left hand and place the Kyanite on your third eye. Allow yourself to relax completely and melt into its gentle vibration. Feel your whole body become ONE with the Crystal energy. As your third eye opens slowly into the pale translucent blue, imagine that you have become a part of the greater Cosmos. Reach upwards to embrace the essence of SPIRIT, allow it to flow down into your body, filling every aspect of your Being. Focus on any part of your physical body that has been causing you discomfort, and direct the essence of SPIRIT to that area. Feel its warmth and its gentle power begin to pulse in that area, embracing and caressing the pain and discomfort, lifting and releasing the emotional and physical bondage that has created it. Now, feel the Light of SPIRIT creating a new vibrancy, a new sense of wellbeing in that area that was discomfort.

Focus now on any other area of your body that needs the gentle embrace of SPIRIT healing, and allow that healing to occur.

With your physical body in balance and harmony you are better able to open yourself to the higher vibrations of energy that are currently flowing into your Dimension. Now, allow yourself to flow into the embrace of the Cosmos, and absorb those powerful new vibrations.

It is time, once more, to resume your journey in the Earth Dimension, bringing to that journey a new perspective on healing and a new empathy with the higher aspects of your Soul Self.

Focus once more on your breathing. Breathe in, hold, breathe out. Breathe in, hold, breathe out. As you breathe out, send the healing energies of SPIRIT out into the room and out into every living plant and creature in your Earth Dimension, for each needs to experience and align with the higher vibrational energies that will create the tomorrow of your World.

All are now ONE with my child the Kyanite.

I am SPIRIT.

SPIRIT of Crystals and Gemstones.

Blessings be upon you.

13

LAPIS LAZULI

Greetings

I am SPIRIT

SPIRIT of Crystals and Gemstones

I come before you in true Light and Infinite Love to share and guide your exploration of the wondrous beauty of my Earthly Children, the Crystals.

Each Crystal is a unique vibration, and each has its own Guardian to direct its work in the Earth Dimension, but all Crystals are ONE with SPIRIT.

I ask you now to relax and place your attention on the Crystal you hold in your left hand.

Focus on your breathing. Breathe in, hold, breathe out. Breathe in, hold, breathe out. As you breathe in,

imagine you are inhaling the essential regal blue of the night sky. As you breathe out, allow all that is limiting and repressing to your Spiritual growth to flow freely from your Being. Breathe in the essential regal blue, breathe out the limiting of your Spiritual growth.

Feel a greater connection, communication, and understanding begin to grow between your emotional and mental aspects. You have now joined the vibration of the Lapis Lazuli.

Within everyone lies an essence comprised of physical, mental and Spiritual energies. Many things in your Dimension distract you from devoting time to harmonizing those energies, resulting in imbalance, illness, depression, and even doubts about the very purpose of your existence. My child the Lapis Lazuli can help you become more in touch with your essence, and play a more active role in the control of your existence. The establishment of a good connection between the emotions and the mind opens many wonderful possibilities. It expands horizons and increases one's potential.

Lapis Lazuli gives you courage, and the fearless adventurous spirit needed to realize your dreams.

Once you see your dreams, and have the feeling they can be achieved, you draw the resources to you that are necessary to attain those dreams. My child helps you to know and accept this as a reality of your life.

The vibratory rate of the Lapis Lazuli itself aligned with the vibratory rate of its deep royal blue colour has the effect of reminding people of the energy, or Spirit, that connects them with the Source, the God power. It has therefore been known through the ages as the 'Messenger of Heaven'. Let us share that connection with the Source now.

Breathe slowly and deeply. Feel your inner self begin to expand so that instead of being contained within your physical body, your inner self now surrounds your physical body. A new sensation of lightness flows through you as you realize you have assumed a new Dimension of existence, one no longer constrained by the denseness of the physical world. Allow yourself to float upwards, to move unhindered around the room. Not apart from your body, but still as ONE with it. Think of a place beyond the room, and immediately you have moved to that place, still as ONE with your physical form. Think of the room again, and you have returned.

You are experiencing the infinite power that lies within yourself. It can be used wisely, or it can be abused, that choice will always be yours to make. For the moment, however, let us journey together through the deep blue night sky to share the wondrous healing, enlightened energy of the ancient Pyramids of Egypt. Time, the elements, and the corruption of mankind, have all served to ravage the beauty that once was, but nothing can diminish the purity and power of their energy. Experience them now, not as physical structures, but as energy structures. Move around them and move inside them, become a part of their incredible wisdom, for they are doorways to the Source. Sit quietly at the Heart point of the Pyramid and open yourself to the God Force of True Light.

Now that you have been filled with the Light and Love of the Source, place your mind once more on the room where your journey began. Allow your inner self to draw slowly back into your physical body, caressing it, and filling, it with the wondrous energies you have experienced in your travels.

Focus once more on your breathing. Breathe in, hold, breathe out. Breathe in, hold, breathe out. Now, as you breathe out, send the Light and Love energy of the Pyramids out to empower all the other Light workers throughout the World.

All are now ONE with my child the Lapis Lazuli.

I am SPIRIT.

SPIRIT of Crystals and Gemstones.

Blessings be upon you.

14

MOONSTONE

Greetings

I am SPIRIT

SPIRIT of Crystals and Gemstones

I come before you in true Light and Infinite Love to share and guide your exploration of the wondrous beauty of my Earthly Children, the Crystals.

Each Crystal is a unique vibration, and each has its own Guardian to direct its work in the Earth Dimension, but all Crystals are ONE with SPIRIT.

I ask you now to relax and place your attention on the Crystal you hold in your left hand.

Focus on your breathing. Breathe in, hold, breathe out. Breathe in, hold, breathe out. As you breathe

in, allow the soft, soothing essence of the Moon to permeate every aspect of your Being. As you breathe out, allow the rigid emotional constrictions in your life to melt and fade slowly away. Breathe in the soft, soothing essence of the Moon, breathe out the emotional constrictions.

Feel yourself becoming more and more in tune with, and in control of, your emotions. You have now joined the vibration of the Moonstone.

As its given name suggests, my child the Moonstone reflects and responds to the nurturing vibration of the Moon itself, bringing to its wearer the gentle, yet powerful energies that control the oceans without, and the oceans within. It helps your higher self harness your emotions, so that you can grow more towards the Light of SPIRIT. By working to calm the emotions and create an openness about Spiritual matters, my child the Moonstone can act as a link so that your Guides can communicate with you more easily, and help you to understand the true nature of your life's path.

Mankind has chosen to represent the emotions as a feminine aspect of Being, and to see the Moon and its attendant Crystal as a powerful influence on that particular aspect. This has sometimes led the male of the species to be uncomfortable with, and even fear, the gentle, powerful Moon based energies that my child reflects, and that is of great sadness to me. For each Being, male or female, needs to establish balance and harmony within themselves, and that means accepting and embracing their emotional aspect as much as their logical and Spiritual aspects.

Now, allow yourself to relax totally, placing your Crystal on your solar plexus, to become ONE with your emotional Being. Feel your body begin to respond to a new, gentle rhythm, as Moonbeams reach down to surround you and embrace you. Feel yourself being drawn slowly upwards through the velvet blue of the night sky, to become part of the Moon itself. Allow yourself to experience the many faces it shows to your Planet as it traverses its eternal cycle, the hope of new beginnings reflected in the new Moon, the energies of abundance and fullness as reflected at its zenith, the inner dreams and acceptance of death as a prelude to rebirth reflected in its waning. Experience all these things in gentle Love.

Now, share your loving, healing energies with the Moon, giving it an equal measure of empowerment to that which you have received, for ALL must be in balance. Join with the Moon in sending Love and Light to your Planet through its emotional centre, the Oceans. Ask for them to be balanced and healed.

Slowly, gently, allow the Moonbeams to carry you back to your physical Dimension, bringing with you an understanding that the Moon speaks to the wholeness of your Being, to the strength of the feminine and the gentleness of the masculine, to the balance of ONENESS.

Focus once more on your breathing. Breathe in, hold, breathe out. Breathe in, hold, breathe out. Now, as you breathe out, fill your room with beams of gentle, nurturing Light. Let them dance Joyfully out into the World with their message of harmony and balance.

All are now ONE with my child, the Moonstone.

I am SPIRIT.

SPIRIT of Crystals and Gemstones.

Blessings be upon you.

15

PYRITE

Greetings

I am **SPIRIT**

SPIRIT OF CRYSTALS AND GEMSTONES

I come before you in true Light and infinite Love to share and guide your exploration of the wondrous beauty of my Earthly children, the Crystals.

Each Crystal is a unique vibration, and each has its own guardian to direct its work within the Earth Dimension, but all Crystals are **ONE** with **SPIRIT**.

I ask you now to relax and place your attention on the Crystal you hold in your left hand.

Focus on your breathing. Breathe in, hold, breathe out. Breathe in, hold, breathe out. As you breathe in,

feel your whole body being filled with the golden rays of the midday sun. As you breathe out, imagine all your anxieties and frustrations melting away. Breathe in the golden rays of the midday sun, breathe out your anxieties and frustrations.

A feeling of joyous upliftment wells up from deep within your being. You have now joined the vibration of the **PYRITE.**

My child the Pyrite is the Sun's messenger to the Earth Planet, shining forth and illuminating everything with a clear, brilliant Light, allowing each person to see with clarity their own individual talents, abilities, skills and gifts, and encouraging them to use those talents wisely. By creating balance between the two aspects of the brain, my child the Pyrite facilitates communication between the creative and intuitive impulses, and the logical and practical impulses. This creates a unique stability within which the individual's talents can more easily unfold.

By helping to create this balance within the mental aspect of your being, my child the Pyrite opens the way for communication with other realms and other Dimensions, facilitating psychic development and enhancing the ability to Channel. In conjunction with my child the Amethyst, it helps to ground spiritual and psychic understanding within the Earth Dimension, leading to a greater affinity between your physical, your mental and your Soul aspects.

Now, slowly raise your left hand, and place the Crystal on your solar plexus Chakra. Feel the gentle, warming rays of the Sun relaxing your total Being. The denseness of your physical Dimension slowly melts away, and you find yourself floating in a sea of Light. Feel yourself becoming **ONE** with the **LIGHT**. Know that there are no longer any limitations, you are free to move within or between Dimensions, free to explore the vast universe of your Soul, free to communicate with Light Beings of other Dimensions and free to communicate in thought form with others in your own Dimension. Take a moment to explore and enjoy these inter - Dimensional Highways of Light.

Although my child the Pyrite facilitates this communication with other Dimensions, its primary role is within your own Dimension. It brings the Light of the Sun to bear on the darkness that mankind has created. Like the beacon of a Lighthouse, it seeks to guide and protect mankind by illuminating those areas of life that pose the greatest danger to the balance and growth of the Earth Planet. Draw the Light of the Sun into yourself and empower it with your deepest spiritual Love. Now, focus on an area of the Planet that is currently in turmoil, locked in the arms of darkness. Send forth your beams of empowered **LIGHT** to that area, surround it, illuminate it, ask that the eyes, minds and Hearts of the Beings in that area be opened by the **LIGHT** and opened to the **LIGHT.** Imagine the mantle of darkness begin to waver and fade as the power of your **LOVING LIGHT** resonates within the hearts of those involved, creating a new awareness, a new understanding and a new respect, one for the other. Hold the focus with all the power of your **LIVING SUN.**

Now it is time once more to return to your physical Dimension, bringing with you the joyfulness of the healing you have just shared with your brothers and sisters elsewhere on your Planet.

Focus once more on your breathing. Breathe in, hold, breathe out. Breathe in, hold, breathe out. As you breathe out, let your inner Sun radiate throughout your Aura, that you may **LIVE IN LIGHT CONSTANTLY.**

All are now **ONE** with my child the **PYRITE**

I am **SPIRIT**

SPIRIT OF CRYSTALS AND GEMSTONES

Blessings be upon you.

16

ROSE QUARTZ

Greetings

I am SPIRIT

SPIRIT of Crystals and Gemstones

I come before you in true Light and Infinite Love to share and guide your exploration of the wondrous beauty of my Earthly Children, the Crystals.

Each Crystal is a unique vibration, and each has its own Guardian to direct its work in the Earth Dimension, but all Crystals are ONE with SPIRIT.

I ask you now to relax and place your attention on the Crystal you hold in your left hand.

Focus on your breathing, breathe in, hold, breathe out. Breathe in, hold, breathe out. As you breathe

in, imagine you are inhaling a gentle pink cloud. As you breathe out, imagine all the tension and stress flowing from your body. Breathe in the pink cloud, breathe out your stress and tension.

Feel your body becoming lighter and lighter. Feel the denseness lift from your Being as you become ONE with the pink cloud. You have now joined the vibration of the Rose Quartz.

Lift your Crystal to your Heart, for it is to the Heart that the Rose Quartz speaks. Take a moment to attune yourself to the particular Crystal that has chosen to be with you tonight and that you have chosen to share your Heart with, for it is, indeed, a mutual decision. Both you and the Crystal are drawn together for each to contribute to the other's growth. This applies to all Crystals, but is especially so for those that relate on an emotional level. Embrace your Crystal in silent affirmation of your inter-dependence.

The essence of your wellbeing is how you see yourself in relation to your immediate environment, and this is controlled by how you feel about yourself. Rose Quartz will work with you in a gentle, subtle way to uplift and enhance your view of yourself by increasing the vibration of Love within your Heart. Love of yourself, and Love and tender appreciation of all things. As your Heart is filled with the healing solace of the Rose Quartz, you can then let that Love flow outwards to others, and begin to recreate your environment in a warmer, more loving, image.

Enfold yourself and your Crystal in the gossamer pink cloud you created earlier, and allow yourself to flow gently upwards until you can look down and see the whole panorama of your life laid out before you. Perhaps you are surprised at the many twists and turns it has taken, at the many peaks and troughs that line its course. There will be parts of your journey that shine brightly like beacons of Light, others that are hidden in swirling mists of tormented darkness. Each has contributed to your current perception of your own self worth. Although we cannot change the events of our journey, we can send loving Rose Quartz energy to those areas of misty darkness that prevent us from seeing ourselves in our true beauty. Send that energy now. Ask that it surrounds the darkness with the Light of Forgiveness, for as we forgive ourselves we sow the seeds of Love within ourselves.

As you look again at the intricate woven pattern of your life and see the swirling mists begin to take on a pinkish glow, begin to lift and float upwards to link with your Crystal cloud, you feel the inflow of Loving Energy, feel the empowerment of your own forgiveness. You begin to vibrate on a new, higher frequency, reaching out to embrace the Divinity within yourself.

Now, turn aside from the panorama of your life, leaving the Rose Quartz to work its gentle nurturing on what has been. Look instead to the journey yet to be undertaken. How you feel about yourself will colour your world as much in the future as it has in the past. There will always be trials and challenges to meet, how you deal with them is as much a product of the Heart as it is of the mind. By having my child the Rose Quartz as your friend and companion, you will be better able to understand and resolve problems so that the Heart is better able to know Love. For the Heart that knows Love will replace feelings of sorrow, fear and resentment with a sense of personal fulfilment and Peace. Rose Quartz promotes the vibrations of Universal Love and inner Serenity, and the world of tomorrow will be much in need of those vibrations. You can be in Harmony with those vibrations by nurturing your own Heart, by feeling Love for yourself, and allowing that Love to flow unconditionally to others.

It is important to recognize that Rose Quartz is not an external agent, it works only from within the self, then flows outwards. You cannot use Rose Quartz to create or command Love in anyone else. You can only create the Love within yourself. However, by creating that Love vibration, you will attract like vibrations into your life, for Love energies flow to Love energies. So, Rose Quartz will help you create a more loving and harmonious environment for the journey that is still to come.

It is time now to reconnect with your Earth Dimension. Bring your pink cloud slowly downwards, embracing and then penetrating your awaiting body. Feel the Crystal energy flow into your Heart, then spread slowly throughout your body, carrying its message of SELF LOVE to every fibre of your Being. Let your new Lightness soften the rigid patterns of the past stored within your physical body, feel a new sense of Joy and wellbeing surge through you, rejuvenating your body, repainting your Aura with a Rainbow of Loving Light.

Focus once more on your breathing. Breathe in, hold, breathe out. Breathe in, hold breathe out. Now, as you breathe out, allow that beautiful pink Loving energy that you have created within your body to flow outwards to embrace all the people within the room, to embrace the Earth itself and all the creatures on it, so that ALL are ONE with the Loving Energy of my child the Rose Quartz.

I am SPIRIT.

SPIRIT of Crystals and Gemstones.

Blessings be upon you.

17

RUBY

Greetings

I am **SPIRIT**

SPIRIT OF CRYSTALS AND GEMSTONES

I come before you in true Light and infinite Love to share and guide your exploration of the wondrous beauty of my Earthly Children, the Crystals.

Each Crystal is a unique vibration, and each has its own guardian to direct its work within the Earth Dimension, but all Crystals are **ONE** with **SPIRIT.**

I ask you now to relax and place your attention on the Crystal you hold in your left hand.

Focus on your breathing. Breathe in, hold, breathe out. Breathe in, hold, breathe out. Imagine yourself immersed in a soft cloud tinted red by the setting sun. As you breathe in, fill your whole being with the gentle red rays. As you breathe out, feel all the tiredness and sluggishness lift from your body and mind. Breathe in the gentle red rays, breathe out all sluggish feelings.

Feel yourself becoming enlivened and energised, awakening to the true essence of your inner self. You have now joined the vibration of the **RUBY.**

My child the Ruby carries within it the true vibration of the red ray, a vibration not of power, as some have perceived it in the past, but a vibration of deep, endearing Love. It seeks to awaken within you a deeper understanding and acceptance of a Love that is beyond the physical, beyond the emotional, a Love that exists within the Divine aspect of your Being. It is not Human Love, for Human Love implies needs and expectations, it is a Love that speaks of freedom, a Love that turns your attention to that which is greater than yourself.

Humans need Love. They need Human Love, yet Human Love alone does not sustain them, because it does not provide their emotional bodies or their inter personal relationships with enough nourishment.

Humans also need **DIVINE LOVE**. My child the Ruby helps you to understand and achieve this state of Divine Love, it will open your heart and give you a taste of what Divine Love is. Then it will show you how to be a vehicle through which Divine Love can enter your life. This Love will then touch others around you, and they will learn from your living example.

Divine Love gives individuals the freedom to be who they really want to be. This freedom nourishes them and their relationships. It gives them space to grow. Divine Love says "I will Love you regardless of what you do, I will Love you regardless of who you are, I will Love you simply because you are **YOU**".

My child the Ruby is also a bridge between your emotional and physical aspects. It empowers the mind to create the opportunities in your life that will allow you to become more in tune with your emotions. It will also help to relax any hold you may have on rigid patterns, melting them away with the warmth of its red vibration, so that necessary changes can be made in your life.

Now, allow your body to relax completely. Lift the Ruby to your Heart Chakra. Feel your breathing become centered in that area. Imagine the red cloud drawn in by your breath begin to pulse and grow, expanding your Heart Chakra. Feel yourself being filled with an overwhelming sense of deep Love. Feel yourself melting into its gentle embrace. Deeper and deeper you move, from the subtle pink glow of the Human Love Dimension, through the deepening red of the Ruby essence to the exquisite purple of the Spiritual Dimension, **THE REALMS OF DIVINE LOVE**. You find yourself in a Temple, its walls adorned with colourful tapestries. This is the **TEMPLE OF YOUR SOUL**. Within it you will find all the Karmic records of your many lives in this and other Dimensions.

The vibrant Tapestries reflect the events of those lives and your emotional responses to them. View the Tapestries one by one, see where your responses have been the product of Human Love, and where they have been the product of Divine Love. There is no judgment of right or wrong, only a growing awareness of the different outcomes that each choice provides. Now, sit quietly in the centre of your Temple and allow the Divine Light of your Soul to filter into the very essence of your Being, bringing you wisdom and understanding, filling you with the unique vibration of **LOVE DIVINE**.

Feel your **ONENESS** with the Love of **GOD.**

Now it is time to leave the Temple of your Soul and journey gently back through the purple, through the red and through the pink, to the welcoming embrace of your Heart Chakra. Bringing with you a clearer understanding of **HUMAN LOVE,** and **DIVINE LOVE**, and the choices you have in your current existence.

Focus once more on your breathing. Breathe in, hold, breathe out. Breathe in, hold, breathe out. As you breathe out, fill your Aura with the exquisite vibration of **DIVINE LOVE**. Make this vibration a part of the permanent fabric of your Aura, and consciously project it out into the world, touching those you know, and those you do not know with the equality and understanding of your **DIVINE LOVE**.

All are now **ONE** with my child the **RUBY**

I am **SPIRIT**

SPIRIT OF CRYSTALS AND GEMSTONES

Blessings be upon you.

18

SODALITE

Greetings

I am SPIRIT

SPIRIT of Crystals and Gemstones

I come before you in true Light and Infinite Love to share and guide your exploration of the wondrous beauty of my Earthly Children, the Crystals.

Each Crystal is a unique vibration, and each has its own Guardian to direct its work in the Earth Dimension, but all Crystals are ONE with SPIRIT.

I ask you now to relax and place your attention on the Crystal you hold in your left hand.

Focus on your breathing. Breathe in, hold, breathe out. Breathe in, hold, breathe out. As you breathe

in, feel your Aura being filled with the deepest blue of the Cosmos. As you breathe out, imagine all the restricting mental patterns of the past lifting and floating away. Breathe in the deep blue of the Cosmos, breathe out the old mental patterns.

Feel the conflict between the conscious and the sub conscious mind being replaced with a new sense of inner harmony. You have now joined the vibration of the Sodalite.

Often ignored and overlooked, the mottled appearance of my child the Sodalite belies its power and importance in the wellbeing of the Earth Planet and the creatures that roam its surface. Joint carrier of the Indigo colour Ray with its brother the Indigo Gemstone, Sodalite acts as a cleanser and purifier of the Earth atmosphere and of the personal atmosphere of the individual, the Aura. Once a person's Aura is less polluted, the Light of SPIRIT can shine through the inner bodies to the physical body more brightly. This enables people to see themselves more clearly, to see who they are, what their strengths and shortcomings are, and in what direction they are headed.

Once these things are known, people can choose to enhance their attributes, work on their shortcomings, or change direction in their lives. Sodalite helps you therefore to remove any clouds of disharmony from your mind by creating a state of balance within it.

Because Sodalite works to clear garbage from the Aura, you are more able to see your own true thoughts, feelings, goals and dreams, and distinguish them from those projected onto you by others. It also works to protect you from any negative thoughts, emotions and other energies directed towards you by others.

Allow yourself to relax completely. Tilt your head back slightly then place your piece of Sodalite on your third Eye, and allow it to sit there. Feel your third Eye opening and awakening. Imagine a tunnel of swirling deep blue Light linking you to the essence of the Universe. Within my child the Sodalite are many soft white clouds. They are your chariots for your journey to the inner wisdom of the Cosmos. Seat yourself upon a cloud and allow yourself to flow down the deep blue tunnel and out into the Universe.

Look down upon your Planet Earth, it is beautiful, is it not?, it is worthy of your Love and of your protection, but like your own Aura, its atmosphere is much in need of the healing qualities of my child the Sodalite. It is important to realize that air pollution can be caused as much by disharmonious thought energies as by the physical pollutants that mankind has created, so there is a primary need for each individual to strive for harmony within their minds and their Auras, then allow that cleaner energy to flow out into the Earth's atmosphere. For the moment, however, enjoy your view of your Planet, send it Loving Light, then move on to explore the wisdom that your Galaxy has to offer. Take your chariot to other Planets and to other Star systems, giving each the benefit of your Loving, healing Light, and accepting from each the joyful wisdom they have to offer you.

Time now to draw your journey to a close, and return once more to the boundaries of your own Planetary Dimension. I hope you have gained a little understanding of yourself in relation to the Universe, for only by understanding your ONENESS with it will you begin to work towards its healing.

Allow your soft white cloud to flow gently back along the deep blue tunnel to reunite you with your physical body. As you do, feel the aspects of both the logical and the Spiritual within you begin to forge a new unity of purpose, bringing your left brain and your right brain into a greater state of harmonious cooperation.

Focus once more on your breathing, Breathe in, hold, breathe out. Breathe in, hold, breathe out. Now, as you breathe out, fill your Aura with the unpolluted Light of the Cosmos, expanding your Aura to encompass the whole room, cleansing it of all physical, mental and emotional pollutants.

All is now ONE with my child the Sodalite.

I am SPIRIT.

SPIRIT of Crystals and Gemstones.

Blessings be upon you.

19

TIGER'S EYE

Greetings

I am SPIRIT

SPIRIT of Crystals and Gemstones

I come before you in true Light and Infinite Love to share and guide your exploration of the wondrous beauty of my Earthly Children, the Crystals.

Each Crystal is a unique vibration, and each has its own Guardian to direct its work in the Earth Dimension, but all Crystals are ONE with SPIRIT.

I ask you now to relax and place your attention on the Crystal you hold in your left hand.

Focus on your breathing. Breathe in, hold, breathe out. Breathe in, hold, breathe out. As you breathe in,

imagine your aura being flooded with the vibrant golden brown of a desert sunrise, allow it to filter slowly into your innermost Being. As you breathe out, feel the energies of negativity and uncertainty being lifted and expelled from your system. Breathe in the golden brown sunrise, breathe out the negativity and uncertainty.

Feel a new sense of personal confidence and inner strength being created within yourself. You have now joined the vibration of the Tiger's Eye.

My child the Tiger's Eye has great power, enabling all who draw near its aura to tap into their own inner power and then use it wisely. It integrates the heat, passion and glaring truth of the sun with the receptive, dark, cool fertility of the earth. From this unification within yourselves comes both inner power and the ability to nurture and create with that power, for it facilitates the integration and balance of the male and female energies within you.

Because of its ever changing appearance when viewed from different angles, the Tiger's Eye helps you to become "all seeing", emphasizing the many different ways of looking at problems and the many different ways of projecting your own image to others. It helps you to recognize the resources within yourself and to use those resources for the attainment of your dreams. It also helps you to judge a situation and determine how best to approach and deal with that situation. But most of all, my child the Tiger's Eye promotes greater Spiritual understanding.

Now, feel the energy of the Crystal in your left hand begin to create within you a new and unique rhythm, combining the gentle throbbing of the earth with the vibrant pulsations of the Sun. Imagine yourself being drawn by this primitive rhythm deep into the lands of the living Dreamtime. Look around you at the stark beauty of the desert landscape, absorb its pristine essence, feel its innate Spirituality, embrace its healing stillness.

See before you a pool of sparkling clear water nestled beneath a craggy outcrop of sun bleached rock. Feel the special vibration of Spiritual Love and Healing that flows forth from this place.

Look closer, there is a gathering taking place, a gathering of Light Beings from many Dimensions, Elders of the Spirit world communing with elders of your Dimension. You have been invited to take your place in this circle of Harmony, to share their wisdom and to contribute your own. Move forward and open your Heart, that each Being present might embrace the truth within you. The Spiritual Elders direct your attention to the mirror surface of the Crystal pool, onto which are projected images of the Planet on which you live, the way it was, the way it is, and the way it could be. You are asked to view them, not with your eyes, or with your mind, but with your Heart. And you are asked to consider how best you can contribute to the Planet's much needed healing. Consider that now.

As the Sun lifts higher into the pale blue sky, its rays sparkle on the gold and red striations of the rock face above the pool, and you recognize the presence of my child the Tiger's Eye, and know that it is time to return from this Sacred place to begin a new relationship with your Planet and with your fellow Light Beings. Give thanks to the Elders that have shared their love and their wisdom with you this day, and move gently back into your conscious Dimension.

Focus once more on your breathing. Breathe in, hold, breathe out. Breathe in, hold, breathe out. Now, as you breathe out, embrace your Planet with the warm radiance of the Sun energies that exist deep within your own Being, allow them to nurture the fertile seeds of change that wait to be awakened in your beautiful Planet.

All is now ONE with my child the Tiger's Eye.

I am SPIRIT.

SPIRIT of Crystals and Gemstones.

Blessings be upon you.

20

TURQUOISE

Greetings

I am SPIRIT

SPIRIT of Crystals and Gemstones

I come before you in true Light and Infinite Love to share and guide your exploration of the wondrous beauty of my Earthly Children, the Crystals.

Each Crystal is a unique vibration, and each has its own Guardian to direct its work in the Earth Dimension, but all Crystals are ONE with SPIRIT.

I ask you now to relax and place your attention on the Crystal you hold in your left hand.

Focus on your breathing. Breathe in, hold, breathe out. Breathe in, hold, breathe out. As you breathe in,

imagine the sea and the sky becoming ONE within your Aura. As you breathe out, allow any negative thoughts to fade from your mind. Breathe in the sea and the sky, breathe out the negative thoughts.

Feel your whole Being become attuned to the life force energies around and within you. You have now joined the vibration of the Turquoise.

No Crystal has greater empathy with the individual than my child the Turquoise, not only does it absorb and reflect the energy of those who wear it, it also teaches the wearer to be more sensitive to the feelings and qualities of those around them. It helps a person to realize that there are no boundaries between them and others. Turquoise greatly encourages us to become ONE with all life, and with the Universe. Its ability to promote empathy and understanding of other people's energy helps those involved in any form of energy based healing.

Allow the gentle vibration of the Turquoise to transport you to a place of infinite serenity and harmony, a moment in space and time where Heaven and Earth become a single reality. This is not a place of dreams and illusions, but a Dimension of reality that gives you the opportunity to see yourself as you are. It is the meeting place of your physical self with your Divine Self, the source and fountainhead of all your wisdom. Bathed in the glow of soft, pulsating Light, feel the power and strength of your Spiritual Self refreshing and rekindling the Light energies within your physical body.

Imagine yourself floating, as if in suspended animation, in this gentle ocean of serene Light. A circle of translucent green moving slowly from your feet to your head, caressing you with Spiritual Love. Then a circle of translucent pale blue moving slowly in the opposite direction. from your head to your feet, caressing you with the wisdom of SPIRIT. As each traverses your body, embrace the essence of their joyful vibration, fill yourself with their Light and their Love.

As you begin to harmonize with these pulsating circles of Light, the vibration of your own Aura intensifies and experiences a subtle transformation, creating as part of its fabric a sheath of pure Gold through which no negative forces can pass without being transmuted into energy beneficial to your Higher Soul Self. The greater the Harmony within yourself, and between yourself and the essence of SPIRIT Light, the more powerful becomes your protective sheath of Golden Light. Allow that Harmony to grow within your ocean of serene Light.

As the circles of green and blue Light move out of your Auric field and fade into infinity. it is time to return your consciousness to your physical Dimension, bringing with you the Harmony and ONENESS you have just created within yourself.

Focus once more on your breathing. Breathe in, hold, breathe out. Breathe in, hold breathe out. As you breathe out, allow the Gold Light within your Aura to bathe the room that you are in, so it too may be empowered to transmute any unwelcome energies that may be directed to it.

All are now within the protective embrace of my child the Turquoise.

I am SPIRIT.

SPIRIT of Crystals and Gemstones.

Blessings be upon you.

21

UNIKITE

Greetings

I am **SPIRIT**

SPIRIT OF CRYSTALS AND GEMSTONES

I come before you in true Light and infinite Love to share and guide your exploration of the wondrous beauty of my Earthly children, the Crystals.

Each Crystal is a unique vibration, and each has its own guardian to direct its work within the Earth Dimension, but all Crystals are **ONE** with **SPIRIT.**

I ask you now to relax and place your attention on the Crystal you hold in your left hand.

Focus on your breathing. Breathe in, hold, breathe out. Breathe in, hold, breathe out. Imagine the subtle pink of dawn's Light caressing the gentle green of a mountain meadow. As you breathe in, allow the fusion of those colours to flow deeply to the centre of your Heart Chakra. As you breathe out, allow any feelings of pain or hurt to lift from your Heart. Breathe in the subtle pink and green, breathe out the pain and hurt.

Feel a new sense of balance and stability fill your whole being. You have now joined the vibration of the **UNIKITE**.

My child the Unikite speaks to the Heart in a deep and sensitive way, embracing it and empowering it with rich earthy energies. Opening the Heart to the acceptance of Loving energies from others by creating within it greater feelings of self worth. It is a crystal of gentle transformation, in oneness with the rhythm of the natural environment. It transmutes feelings of self hatred into feelings of self Love, feelings of self doubt into feelings of self confidence, feelings of worthlessness into feelings of worthiness, in such a subtle way that the balance and harmony of the individual is never threatened.

As self esteem grows, my child the Unikite works to promote the acceptance and the expression of your deepest Heart felt needs and desires. It promotes also the realization of your own Divine worth, your own equality in Light. The duality of its colour vibration symbolises the **EARTH** and the **SPIRIT** together in rich **ONENESS**, together in the embrace of **LOVE**.

Imagine you are lying in the middle of that green mountain meadow, the pink rays of the early morning sun warmly caressing your face. Allow yourself to relax into that warmth, your whole being melting into the embrace of the Earth. Feel a deep sense of **ONENESS** with **ALL THAT IS**, a deep sense of tranquil Joy. Feel yourself becoming a part of the fabric of Mother Earth, moving deeper and deeper into its vibrant Heart Chakra. Feel your own Heart Chakra begin to pulsate with a new, deeper, more powerful vibration, as waves of green and pink Healing Light wash through you. It is as if you are being purified within the Earth itself. Reach out and embrace the healing of Mother Earth, open and accept the Love it has to share with you.

Now from the Love essence of your own Being, send out the healing Light from within your Heart, to give as you have received. Embrace Earth Mother with the Light of your unconditional Love.

Each has given, each has received, in **TRUE LIGHT** and **INFINITE LOVE,** and it is time once more to return to your physical Dimension, taking with you a greater understanding of your **ONENESS** with the Planet on which you live.

Focus once more on your breathing. Breathe in, hold, breathe out. Breathe in, hold breathe out. As you breathe out, let the green and the pink vibration flow gently out into the world, to embrace all life forms within your Dimension with the special Love of **MOTHER EARTH**.

All are now **ONE** with my child the **UNIKITE.**

I am **SPIRIT**

SPIRIT OF CRYSTALS AND GEMSTONES.

Blessings be upon you.

22

CRYSTAL PYRAMID ENERGY THERAPY

Back in 1993 whilst working as part of the EarthMother Centre Beloved Germain gifted to Meredith Pope and myself details of what he termed an ancient Lemurian Crystal Healing technique involving both Crystals and Pyramids, and asked me to obtain 10 clear quartz pyramid Crystals. I ordered them but was disappointed when they came and I saw that they were of varying sizes and angles and therefore not all strictly of the Egyptian pyramid angles which we had been led to believe were 'special'. Germain laughed and said, "Did I say anything about angles? I only said Pyramid shapes, smile, and these would not have been brought to you if they were not intended for you to work with". He was, of course, right, smile. We already had a large Pyramid and for a number of years Meredith and I worked with this Technique and found it to be incredibly powerful. I therefore gift you here the instructions we received from Beloved Germain so you may explore the Crystal Pyramid Healing technique if you feel drawn to do so. **HAVE FUN !!**

David J Adams

Requirements :
One Large (perhaps 8ft high) Pyramid.
One Therapy Table.
10 small Pyramid shaped clear quartz Crystals
One bottle of Australian Bushflower essence, or a Dr Bach remedy that your Heart chooses.
Two Therapists.

Instructions :

Place the Therapy table beneath the large Pyramid, then place the person seeking to receive the Therapy on the table and cover with a light cloth. The head of the person should be facing North.

7 drops of the Special Chakra empowerment Bushflower essence or Dr Bach remedy that your Heart has chosen should be placed under the tongue of the person on the table.

Place one of the small Pyramid shaped Clear Quartz Crystals on each of the 9 major Chakras of the person's body. A tenth Crystal for empowerment of the back of the head Chakra should be placed on the ground beneath the table directly below where the head is placed.

The two Therapists should place themselves one on either side of the person's body at approximately waist level. They should 'activate' the flow of energy by placing their hands in a "W" shape, using the two thumbs together and the two index fingers opened out alongside (representing wellbeing) and touching their hands together across the person's body. This signals the beginning of the Therapy.

One of the Therapists should place themselves on the left side of the person on the table and take hold of their left hand. The left hand is the 'receiver' of energies, and the role of that Therapist is to act as a 'filter' to ensure that only balanced energies of Light are invited in to the person on the table.

The second Therapist should place themselves on the right side of the person on the table and take hold of their right hand. The right hand is the 'giver' of energies, and the role of that Therapist is to 'sense' when the energy being taken in by the left hand has fully completed it's work within the body and all is in balance, and the energy is ready to flow freely from the person on the table. This indicates that the session is over.

Because you are working with very powerful energies with the Two pyramids – the Large Pyramid over the table and the small pyramid Crystals on each chakra – and the Bushflower essence, the MAXIMUM time that the Therapy should be given is 15 MINUTES. Some may cope with or need much less energy than others, so some Therapies may need to be curtailed before the 15 minutes has expired, but **NONE SHOULD EXCEED THAT 15 MINUTES**. The Therapist holding the right hand is the monitor of the energies and will **'FEEL'** when the energy exchange has been completed.

Wait a few moments after the energy completion has taken place then gently help the person from the table and ground the person by both Therapists brushing the aura of the person in a downward direction both back and front, again holding their hands in the "W" shape to acknowledge the wellbeing of the person. Then allow the person to sit for a short period until they feel sufficiently grounded to stand and move around. They may feel a little dizzy at first.

23

GLOBAL CRYSTAL ACTIVATIONS

At the beginning of 1997 the Master Germain announced that it was time to forge a new **'Inter - Dimensional Partnership of Healing'**, to put aside the divisions and isolationism of the past and come together in *'Oneness of Purpose, Oneness of Spirit'*. As part of that process, he called upon all those Souls that had chosen to incarnate within the Crystal Dimension to join with Humanity, and the Souls incarnate within the Ocean Dimension, by adding their Love and Light to this powerful partnership of Healing.

The Souls within the Crystal Dimension responded joyfully to his call and worked powerfully with us in 1997, and their work culminated at the time of the September 23rd Marine Meditation when a massive

Crystal was activated beneath the Ocean in the South Pacific. This Crystal was situated some two and a half hours east of New Zealand and was Pulsing brilliant Blue Light. I was given the awareness that this Crystal formed part of a linking bridge between the crystal energies of Atlantis and Lemuria, activating those ancient Crystal energies for the specific purpose of *'Holding the Earth in Balance'*.

They continued to work with us in 1998 when we were asked by the Master Germain to Honour all life forms in all Dimensions, acknowledging their Equality within the *'All that is'*. But there was a new addition to the team !! the Masters **Hilarion** and **Dwahl Khul** came to stand alongside the Master **Germain** and add their Love and Light to this Partnership of Healing !!. This culminated at the time of the September 23rd Marine Meditation with the activation of a second massive Crystal beneath the Oceans - this time in the Indian Ocean some half an hour East of Madagascar. This Crystal was Pulsing brilliant Violet Light, and I was given the awareness that where the Violet Light from this Crystal met the Blue Light from the 1997 Crystal, a Spiral Energy Vortex would be formed that would be of **great significance to Earth Healing, and**

would be a communication vehicle for the New Christ Consciousness !.

I was also given advance notification that a third massive Crystal would be activated within this Spiral Energy Vortex at some time in the future, and that this third Crystal would be pulsing Gold Light. No specific date was given, but it appeared to me that it would be 'sooner, rather than later !'. What would be formed by the activation of this third Crystal was the **'Threefold Flame of Christ Consciousness' !**

It became clear very quickly that as the Blue and Violet light from the first two crystals would meet at two points around the world, and therefore form two Spiral Energy Vortexes, this third crystal would have to be double terminated and pass right through the centre of the Earth ! It was important, therefore, to seek more specific information on the positioning of these Crystals, so I sat in meditation with Spirit and asked for further guidance. The following information emerged : All three Crystals were activating along the line of the **Tropic of Capricorn** ! : The 1997 Crystal had as its centre of activation the coordinate **143 degrees West** : The 1998 Crystal had as its centre of activation the coordinate **52.5**

degrees East. This meant that the meeting point of the two Crystal energies (the Spiral Energy Vortex) had as its central points coordinates **134.75 degrees East**, and **45.25 degrees West** !.

Transferring this information to world maps provided the information that one termination point would be within **Serra Do Mar (Sea Ranges)** in Brazil, close to the town of **Natividade Da Serra**, and the other termination would be within the **White Ranges** in Central Australia at a place called **Arltunga.**

On 19th December 1998, a group led by **Ana Maria Freitas Silveira** went to the Serra Do Mar and conducted a meditation close to the point of Crystal activation. We in Australia, and a number of other groups around the world, held meditations to empower Ana Maria's group, and as a result, the Third Crystal began to activate !! It's activation was completed at the time of the Solstice on December 22nd !! **At the precise time of the Solstice the Threefold Flame began to pulse its message of Christ Consciousness into the Hearts of every Being on this Planet, and to the Heart of the Earth itself !!!!!**

Although this may seem like an ending, the culmination of the work we had been doing since 1991, **IT WAS ONLY THE BEGINNING !** a platform has been created on a higher frequency level to assist us and the Planet in the Ascension Process. We still need to embrace the new energy and work with the new energy. As always the Masters are there to help us, and Spirit is there to guide us !

The September Equinox Marine Meditation of 1997 saw the awakening/ Activation of the first in a series of Three major Crystal energies, the first Crystal pulsated brilliant Blue Light. The second Crystal was awakened/Activated at the September Equinox Marine Meditation in 1998 pulsating brilliant Violet Light. The third Crystal – which was double terminated and passed right through the Earth – was awakened/Activated at the Solstice of 1998, pulsating brilliant Gold Light

As we were a group operating in the Southern Hemisphere at the time, all three Crystals revealed to us were activated along the line of the tropic of Capricorn in the Southern Hemisphere. It was advised to us at the time that a similar Trinity of Crystals existed in the Northern Hemisphere, but these would be awakened by a group or groups in that part of the world. I have been given no indication of who this group may have been or if, in fact, it happened, but **Beloved Tarak, Sound Master of Arcturus,** has **NOW** advised me that the Crystals in the Northern Hemisphere were/ are located along the Tropic of Cancer at identical Longitude co-ordinates as those that were advised to us along the Tropic of Capricorn. This means that the Crystals in both Hemispheres are located at 143 degrees West (Crystal 1), 52.5 degrees East (Crystal 2), 134.75 degrees East and 45.25 degrees West (The two terminations of Crystal 3).

NOTE - Global positioning of the crystals is as follows:

<u>Southern Hemisphere</u>

Crystal 1, Ocean adjacent to Island of Tahiti … Brilliant Sapphire Blue radiance
Crystal 2, Ocean adjacent to Island of Madagascar … Brilliant Amethyst Purple radiance
Crystal 3, Ocean adjacent Serra do Ma (Brazil) … Brilliant Gold radiance

Area of Arltunga (Central Australia) ... Brilliant Gold radiance

Northern Hemisphere

Crystal 1, Ocean North of Hawaii ... Brilliant Emerald Green radiance

Crystal 2, Area SE of Ryadh, Saudi Arabia ... Brilliant Rose Pink radiance

Crystal 3, Ocean SE of Okinawa, Japan ... Brilliant Silver radiance

Ocean NE of Antigua and Barbuda ... Brilliant Silver radiance

Printed in the United States
by Baker & Taylor Publisher Services